FINDING
PURPOSE
—— in ——
YOUR
PAIN

Former editor of *Christianity Today* and president of Scripture Press, **V. Gilbert Beers** is the author of many books for children including *Precious Moments Through-the-Year Stories* and *The Children's Illustrated Bible Dictionary.*

FINDING PURPOSE

—in—

YOUR PAIN

V. GILBERT BEERS

Published by Fleming H. Revell
a division of Baker Book House Company
P.O. Box 6287, Grand Rapids, MI 49516-6287

Spire edition published 1998

Printed in the United States of America

ISBN 0-8007-8649-1

For current information about all releases from Baker Book House, visit our web site:

http://www.bakerbooks.com

CONTENTS

INTRODUCTION

I never realized how many hurting people surround me all the time until I was hurt deeply. How could I have been so blind? Or am I so unlike my friends and neighbors? Is it possible that most of us meander through life insensitive to the wounds of those quite close to us?

This is a book about the layers of hurts I experienced following my son's fatal automobile accident. As such, it becomes personal, too personal for my comfort, for in a sense I am licking my wounds in public and that in itself is painful. But in revealing my wounds, I trust that I may help you see something in your hurts that you never saw before.

Pain behaves like a pack of wild dogs, surrounding us and driving us into dark corners of ourselves where we seek refuge from the world and nurse our woundedness. And there are so many of us sitting in those dark corners, afraid to deal with our hurts lest we lose our privacy with them.

I know quite a few people who lost money on Black Monday, October 19, 1987, when the Dow Jones index fell 508 points in one day. These were not wealthy people, but had some savings or retirement funds tucked into stocks and suddenly saw their nest eggs broken. Some friends died during the months I have been writing this book. Others faced painful decisions about their mates or children. It seems to me that we always have at least one friend in job turmoil. Some are eased out of their jobs and don't know why. Others are fired abruptly. Some wish they could leave but don't have good options. Still others lose their jobs on the threshold of retirement.

We have friends who struggle with debilitating diseases. Others have heard the awesome word *cancer* and with disbelief have learned that it is they, not their neighbors, who have it. A dear lady we know is dying of cancer and knows it. She has planned her funeral and recognizes that the dark latter days will soon visit her. Another woman has a deteriorating bone disease. She depends on others to feed her.

Have you ever made a list of all the hurts you know surround you? When the list is complete, it will be only a fraction of the hurts that are there. So many are swept under the carpet of our lives. I would be surprised if you don't know at least a half dozen couples in the process of divorce, and at least that many more who are thinking about it.

This book takes you into the inner sanctum of my heart and mind as I have wrestled with my own hurt from my son's death. It is a private struggle. All that is within me says that I do not want to make it public. Some things are too personal to be public.

But I have come to believe that our wounds are for the healing of those about us, and we cannot apply their therapeutic qualities until we are willing to reveal them. I really don't want to do this, but I believe it is the mission of the wounded also to be healers, and like Jesus, it is through our wounds that you may be healed. If I hide my wounds, so may you, and many hurting people may not discover the therapy that our wounds can bring.

This book is a call for you and me to suffer one more layer of pain, the pain of exposing our woundedness. But this time the pain is *for* something, *for* someone.

If you are wounded and wonder why, this is a book for you. If you are wounded and wonder what to do about it, this is for you. If you suffer hurts and wonder which way to go next, I invite you to share in my struggles and hope you find something for your own.

WEAKNESS

Wanting to Fly
When You Can't Even Crawl

Long, cold fingers of an Adirondack night gripped me as I stepped into the phone booth. There was no door, and the wind swirled through its openness recklessly. But this was the last public phone before we reached our rustic cottage on Whitaker Lake, tucked back in the mountains where the phone company had not yet ventured. This was the last opportunity to use a phone that night, and my wife, Arlie, insisted that we must call home now.

We had called home only three days before, so why the urgency? News, significant and trite, had been exhausted then, so what more was there to say now? But those of us who have been married many years learn to trust our mate's instincts, even though at the time they may seem strange, even irrational.

This was our third phone stop. At the first, there was a never-ending busy signal; at the second, a broken phone. Now

I found this last phone would neither produce a dial tone nor return my coins. Disheartened, I hammered on it with my fists, expecting nothing more than mild relief for my frustration. Then to my amazement, a dial tone began!

When our son Ron answered, I started chattering and laughing about the phone system in the Adirondacks, but after patiently listening to my inane babbling for a few seconds he cut me short. "Dad, are you strong?" he asked. "I have some tragic news for you. Doug went to be with the Lord last night in a car accident."

The bone-chilling night air shifted its hand grip to a full embrace. I felt as though a cold shroud was thrown around me, a shroud hiding strong hostile arms that held me tight. Death itself moved into the phone booth, and I felt its chilling presence as never before, sucking something warm and vital from me, offering nothing in return.

Our handsome, bright, promising twenty-six-year-old son had been snatched from us in a moment. We couldn't even say good-bye. And now we were a thousand miles from home and family and couldn't put our arms around the others. How much I wanted to do that—hold each one tight and exchange warmth of presence.

At that moment our lives were radically changed. At that precise point in time we became different people from those who stopped to make a simple phone call. From that point on we would view things through different eyes, and I suppose others would view us from a different perspective too.

As long as I can remember I have watched a steady stream of tragedies sweep across the lives of family and friends. I could compile a rather bulky catalog of these—the woman who grew tired of being wife and mother and ran away with another man, a young neighbor who chose to hang herself in the barn instead of running away, the teen who got in with the wrong friends and had an abortion, the parents who pulled their three-year-old son's body from a family swimming pool, the man who lost his job at age sixty-two and his self-assurance with it. The list is endless. You could make your own list as long as mine, perhaps longer.

But of course these things never happened to me. They always happened to the other person. Those of us who for many years walk unscathed among life's threats and tragedies create two masks—one self-assured, almost smug because "it's never happened to me," the other etched with lines of fear because we feel certain our time will come. My time had come. That night, September 23, 1981, I entered life's infirmary, filled with multitudes of those who have been wounded by forces, often beyond their control, and wonder why. I began a forced pilgrimage on that dark path the psalmist called "the valley of the shadow of death." I joined that endless queue of those who have been hurt and cry out for healing.

In the autumn chill of that Adirondack phone booth I confronted a new presence in my life, the presence of death that embraced my son and me in different ways, but with the same cold, unyielding arms. I also confronted my absolute helplessness to reverse the tragedy, my helplessness to give my son one last embrace, and even my helplessness to say anything truly meaningful to my wife, Arlie. I looked into her worried eyes and blurted out, "Doug was killed in a car accident last night." A total stranger could have done better at that moment in easing the pain of the statement.

Numb and broken, we returned to our cottage, instinctively fell into each other's arms and cried uncontrollably and without shame, until it seemed we could cry no more. We did not need to explain our helplessness or tears to each other.

Arlie knew I was as helpless as she, and I knew she was as help-less as I. Each of us baptized the other's helplessness with our tears. From time to time we punctuated our tears with our prayers. Reflecting on this overwhelming time of weakness later, I thought of Hansel and Gretel, lost in the woods, two helpless little children, out of bread crumbs to mark their path, and suddenly realizing that the crumbs they left were eaten by hungry birds. I related to these little children who were not sure what to do next.

The rest of that sleepless night was spent packing, driving to the nearest airport in Albany, New York, and checking in for the next flight to Chicago. With two hours to flight time it was too late to get a motel and too early to board, so we sprawled out on the hard seats in the waiting room.

But who could sleep? Loud, raucous music blared from the public address system, bombarding us with insipid lyrics about a self-centered love that is there only as long as "the feelings" are there. It was a love that had never walked the path of sacrificial commitment through twenty-six years of strongly bonded husband-wife, parent-child relationships. I wondered how that kind of love would hold up at an hour like this under the lengthening shadows in "the valley of the shadow of death." How might some of these musicians change their tune if their son had just died in an auto accident? Would they sing of a different kind of love, a love that endured beyond the feelings?

The flight home was interminable, a never-ending launch into trackless, uncharted space. I had lost my mother earlier that year and was acquainted with death, but she was ninety-two and we had known for three years that her time was approaching and that she was ready. We had lost what would have become our first grandchild a few months before, but it was a miscarriage of a molar pregnancy, a growth of the placenta, with no fetus. Our bonding was to an expectation, an unrealized hope, rather than to a son of twenty-six years.

Now we were flying toward a new world of wakes and funerals, cemeteries and grave sites, caskets and tombstones, and at the center of all this pageantry of death was a son—a baby we had cuddled, a boy we had embraced, a young man we had encouraged. It was an unreal world of incongruities—the warm, bright, hopeful prospect of sonship and the cold, shadowy, pessimistic desolation of death with all its morbid paraphernalia. The two clashed in the center of our hearts, and the conflicts on those unseen battlefields left deep wounds and scars, no less ugly and painful than those left in days of old by swords and spears.

I longed to return to our living children, yet dreaded it too. While we had vacationed at the charming Queechee Inn in Vermont the night he died, our high-school-age daughter, Cindy, had waited at home, worrying and watching for each passing pair of headlights to turn into our driveway. No one was there with Cindy when the state trooper came to the door without a shred of information for her, adding immeasurably to her worries. What should we say to Cindy?

What should we say to Ron and his wife, Becki, who went out to look for Doug and returned home to cautiously break the news to Cindy that Doug would not be coming home that night, or any night? What should we say to Jan, who received a phone call that night twenty miles away at college, sensing immediately that she was about to hear unwanted news and wondering if something had happened to us? What should we say to our daughter Kathy and her husband, Brad, who joined the others throughout the long night, and all the next day, calling inns throughout Vermont, trying to locate us?

I should not have worried about what to say. I was about to discover an important truth that parents everywhere should know, that we parents can learn much from our children. The wave of helplessness that had swept over me that night had also washed over our children back home. But they, not I, took the first step to turn their helpless state into hope. After calling inns throughout Vermont (except the one where we stayed), and after waiting almost twenty-four hours without results for the Vermont State Police to find us through an all-points bulletin, our children gathered together in the living room and prayed earnestly that God would send us to a telephone. I would learn why Arlie had said so urgently, "We must call home."

And I would remember Michelangelo's powerful painting on the vault of the Sistine Chapel with God's life-giving finger of power about to touch Adam's finger of weakness. It seemed to me that God had the finger of one hand on our praying children that night and the finger of the other hand stretching out a thousand miles to touch Arlie, relaying a prayer message, completing the electric circuit of prayer. No words were sent, but the message got through. Isn't that what intercessory prayer is all about?

TURN YOUR WEAKNESS INTO STRENGTH

Looking at Emptiness as an Opportunity for Filling

The cycles of life are self-perpetuating. You've heard the old saying, "The rich get richer and the poor get poorer"? We could add another, "The weak get weaker and the strong get stronger."

If you've watched many games in the pro leagues, you know how true this is. Players and teams get on a roll, up or down. A team rolling downhill toward defeat faces twice the challenge as the team on a roll toward victory. It can be done, but it's a challenge.

Life is like that. We get on a roll, up or down, and it's tough to reverse the trend. When things start going wrong, there seems to be no letup. When good things start to happen, it seems easy to succeed.

Doug's death started a roll down for us, with a series of pits toward a greater pit. You may now be on a downward roll, and you don't know what to do about it.

Perhaps the lifechangers which helped us will also help you. Life is never static, so you have two options in dealing with a life-weakening situation—let it send you into a downward spiral of increasing weakness or turn your weakness into strength.

Lifechanger 1
Life at its best is an adventure. To live the adventure you must risk getting hurt, for only through the adventure of living will you grow strong.

It is pointless to ask if you or I will be hurt. This is a hostile world, and we are vulnerable people, so we must expect to be wounded. We *will* get hurt sometime! No one is immune to hurts. We may be tempted to think, "It will always happen to the other person, not to me," but that is not realistic. We will meet hurts face to face in life's road. There is no way to avoid them. There is no detour around them.

Even so, ours is an exciting world because life is filled with opportunities for adventures. Some people fill life with high adventures, full of risk. Others choose the stuff of everyday living, with only modest risk, but even that can be done with a spirit of adventure. All living, and all adventure, carries with it a risk of getting hurt. Live a full, rich, delightful life and you will get hurt now and then.

What your hurts will be I do not know. You will not know either until they stare you in the face, eyeball to eyeball. Your hurts may be smaller than mine, a misunderstanding with someone you love, financial loss, or damaged property. They may be even greater. They may come like ours, in a split second, with no time to plan or correct course. Or they may come as they did to our friends Harris and Alice Hanson, whose daughter Sheloa, about Doug's age, died slowly of cancer over several months.

The timeliness of pain does not determine the intensity of pain. Hurts that leap at you without warning are neither more nor less painful than those that require a year or more to wound you.

Harris and I talked about this in a time of reflection, wondering which pain was greater, our wound inflicted without warning or theirs that cut ever more deeply over the passing of time. There are trade-offs. Abruptness brings the added pain of shock, but spares the pain of lingering suffering. Loss that comes slowly grants time to adjust, but it prolongs the suffering. How can we ever know which pain is greater? God's mercy spares us from knowing or choosing some of life's alternatives. We must let God be God in these matters and then trust the way he does it.

Is anyone immune to hurts? No, not one of us. Has anyone lived such a good life that pain and suffering will pass him by? I have not yet met that person. I doubt if you have either.

The question concerning hurts is not if, but what and when and where. A tornado roared across Arkansas recently. People died. Others lost their homes and possessions. One woman stood helplessly between the wreckage of her home and the TV camera and said, "Everything I've ever worked for is gone . . . gone!" This woman can't undo what was done. She can't rescind the wind or weather. All she can do is pick up the broken pieces of her life and try to put something together for the future. But she *can* do that. She still has her life and health.

Some friends lost their ten-month-old granddaughter. I know they felt as helpless as we did when we cried in each other's arms that night in our cottage. They made the same discovery we made, that we cannot undo circumstances. We cannot wish the broken china back into wholeness. We cannot recall the arrow shot into the air or erase the foolish word we spoke to a friend yesterday.

Each deed we do, each word we speak, is stamped with certainty and finality and these make us helplessly aware of our inadequacy. Nothing I say or do will ever change the certainty of my son's death or the finality of it. I stand helpless before these two stoic figures. And I see my own inadequacy, my weakness, mirrored in them.

Most of us have friends and neighbors who have lost their jobs, suffered from debilitating sickness, or faced misunderstanding by friends or family. How many do you know with a deteriorating marriage or a breakdown in parent-child communication? There are so many of these "little" hurts that newspapers and TV ignore them for the most part. But these little hurts are just as painful as those with story value, especially if you are the one who is hurting.

Hurts do not discriminate. They visit black and white, old and young, rich and poor, good and evil alike. No one can ever say, "I suffer more because I am rich (or poor)," or "I suffer less because I am good (or evil)." We may hurt differently, but no more or less. On the night when the angel of death visited Egypt, Pharaoh grieved no more or no less for his dead son than the poorest Egyptian father, even though he grieved in more luxury. But at such a time, luxury is a poor comforter.

We may be tempted to think that we can avoid hurts by avoiding the adventure of living. We could shut ourselves in the closet, lock the door, and throw away the key. Of course, life is not all roses in a dark closet either. The hurt of isolation from life's adventures may be the greatest of all hurts. You and I cannot protect ourselves and our children from all risks. So that is not the answer. I don't want to give up the adventure of living, and neither do you.

I suppose we could stop driving cars or even riding in cars. That would reduce some risk, wouldn't it? But it would certainly reduce the adventure of living too. Imagine telling your twenty-six-year-old son that he shouldn't drive a car because he might get hurt. Imagine telling your twenty-year-old daughter that she can't go on a date because her friend is driving a car and she will have to ride in it. She will probably say, "What are we supposed to do, ride a bike or walk? Accidents happen to bike riders and walkers too, you know." Of course she would be right.

We could stay home. But an unusually high percentage of accidents happen within the home. Many happen in the bathtub. We do have to take baths, so the adventure of keeping clean has its own risk too. Not many of us will stop taking baths because there is a risk that we could get hurt in the bathtub.

When our son Ron was fifteen, he asked if he and his cousin Steve could ride their bikes to upstate New York, an eight-hundred-mile trip. They had planned the itinerary carefully and were strong young men, but Ron would be barely sixteen when they went. Should we let them do it? We knew there were risks, dozens of them. But every exciting adventure is filled with risks. That's what makes it adventure!

We knew we could say no, but we didn't have a good reason, except that they might get hurt. Of course they might also get hurt riding their bikes down the street or around the block. We agonized over the decision and let them go. We have since been glad that we did, for it was a great adventure with much personal growth and nobody got hurt.

Story writers will tell you that there is no story unless the main characters take risks, go on adventures, become vulnerable. High adventure involves greater risk. That's the way stories are and that's the way life is too. When you live life to the fullest, enter into the adventure of living, you are vulnerable, at risk, but none of us wants to relinquish the adventure of living.

Perhaps you are a parent who let your child participate in one of life's adventures and that child was hurt or killed. It's easy to let guilt take over. Your mind is filled with "if only" or "what if" and they nag you. May I remind you that you can't protect your child from everything. Your child could have been hurt on any one of a thousand other adventures necessary to growing up as a child.

Of course there is a point of reasonableness—avoiding risks that are foolish, refusing to let your child take risks that are senseless or out of balance. No thoughtful person would risk life and limb to keep a toy from getting broken. We should teach our children never to risk their lives to save a pet, no matter how much they love it. Jesus reminded us in Matthew 10:31 that our lives are worth more than many sparrows (or hamsters, or cats, or dogs, or whatever).

On balance, we are willing to take the normal risks to live life as God intended us to live it. Foolhardiness is the unnatural desire to take unnecessary and unwarranted risks. But overprotectiveness is the unnatural desire to avoid reasonable risk in order to live the abundant life.

I prefer not to crawl into a hole and pull a lid over it, or go into a dark closet and close the door behind me. I prefer to participate in the undertaking of living as God intended. High risk is not my style, but for some it's just the thing. Will I get hurt living life's adventure? Of course I will. I have. But I will be hurt more if I withdraw from life, a deadening hurt. I want to live God's adventure, with its risks, for that is the kind of world God made for me—and for you.

Lifechanger 2
Hurts are a form of growing pains. Since you want to grow strong, you must be willing to accept the necessary hurts to do it.

For some reason, God's plans for the human experience in this world included suffering. He could have planned life on earth as a pain-free, hurt-free, sickness-free, work-free existence. Imagine yourself in such a sterile world. You can never get hurt, you can never suffer, you can never get sick, you never need to work. Life has no demands, no restraints, no boundaries, no accountability, no limitations.

So why be careful? With no boundaries on my behavior, I can jump from buildings, drive my car into yours on the expressway, hack at you with an ax, do anything I want because you will not feel the pain or suffer the consequences. Of course you should feel free to return the favor!

I really do not want to live in so chaotic a world, do you? In heaven, with its perfect lifestyle, this will work. On earth, with its imperfect people and systems, it will not.

God in his wisdom created hurts to establish boundaries around my life, put restraints on my conduct, provided highways on which I can drive, for through discipline and exercise and restraint, he helps me grow strong. Without the disciplines of work, sweat, tears, and hurts I will not grow.

When our children were born my wife and I committed the rest of our lives to small, and sometimes not so small, acts of sacrificial service for them—walking the floor with a sick child at night, nursing, feeding, bathing, buying food and clothing, coaching, helping them with homework, motivating, loving, giving music lessons, chauffeuring, helping them learn lines for school plays, watching Little League games, attending PTA meetings, faithfully (and sometimes tediously) listening to recitals, and a thousand other activities.

These activities consumed our time, and we could have thought all of this was keeping us from our work. But we knew the children *were* our work because we were parents. And we loved our children more than the other things, and love requires sacrificial involvement.

When Arlie and I were married, and when each child was born, I thought less and less of what I wanted and more and more of what we wanted. So did Arlie. Then I discovered something exciting—what we wanted was much more important to me than what I wanted because "we" had become much more significant to me than "I." What we might call "we-ness" had cost me my "I-ness" but I found it much more enriching to me because the new "me" was in reality "us." Growing into a new relationship with wife and children is costly, because it costs our old self. But its costliness actually becomes one of its own rewards because the new self is more exciting than the old one.

Growing is costly to my children too. Every step of growth cost them something. When Doug went to school he had to give up some playtime and commit himself to study, and that's hard work. When Kathy started music lessons she had to give up some of her free time to practice. When Ron joined Little League he could no longer count on his own hours at home.

Jan and Cindy each had some growth-producing activities and each one cost them something that "I" wanted.

Athletics force a child into rigorous training. Music lessons are meaningless without hours of practice. School is of little value without study time. It is hard to think of any area of growth that doesn't cost.

Growing is a costly pilgrimage toward maturity. Small investments today reap enormous rewards tomorrow. The person who has turned weakness into strength is the one who has accepted the growing pains in order to become a mature man or woman of God.

Small steps in growing stronger are actually giant steps in learning discipleship. A disciple is not a disciple until he learns the discipline of walking in the steps of his master (or coach, teacher, parent, scout leader, and so on), and discipline costs. The small disciplines of life are necessary in learning to be a disciple of Christ. Any attempt to grow as a disciple of Christ without paying a price is, in the words of Dietrich Bonhoeffer, "cheap grace." Jesus' price for grace was not cheap. Ours can't be either.

Lifechanger 3
Understanding why you hurt is less important than trusting the Person who can help you be healed. Building godly relationships will help you much more than seeking answers to your questions.

Researchers say that we live in an information age. I believe it, because we like to explain everything that happens. We are consumed with seeking or giving answers, even when there are no questions. We have developed elaborate hardware and software to manage our information. (I'm using some of it to write this book!) But too often we become so enamored with information and the systems necessary to manage it that we allow it to obscure relationships.

When Doug died, *why* screamed at us. Why should a robust twenty-six-year-old in the prime of his life be taken when we knew older people begging God each day to take them out of their suffering? Why did he precede his father and grandfather in death? Why was he taken at twenty-six instead of eighty-six? Why were the seasons of life disrupted, bringing winter before summer had passed? There was a long line of whys, the unanswerables crying out for answers. Why? Why? Why?

You must have asked why a hundred times, no, a thousand times too. Why was I born white and you were born black? Why was I born poor and you were born in wealth? Why was I born in a free land and you were born in a repressive society? Why did I have to fight on the battlefront and you had a desk job in Hawaii? Why did I miss my flight, the one my neighbor took, the one that crashed without survivors? As in times of war, we may have two sides of a conflicting situation crediting or blaming God for the same act.

Implied in *why* is "Who did it," "Who's to blame?" We sink into a very human tendency to blame or credit someone for everything, when blame or credit may be our most pointless exercise at that moment. Suppose we establish blame or credit and point a finger at God. What do we do then, give him a medal or three demerits? What good would that do?

When I was in high school I played on the football team with a fellow named Bunk Bland. I'm sure Bunk wasn't his given name, but I don't think any of us ever knew what it was. One day Bunk was walking across a cornfield. Somewhere a hunter shot at an animal and the stray bullet struck Bunk. It was a freak accident, one in a hundred million odds that it could happen.

What would I say to my teammate if I had been there in his dying moment and he asked me why? I would feel helpless to explain why. What if he asked if God had guided that stray bullet to him so he would die at that moment? What would I say? I know I would feel an overwhelming weakness in trying to explain what had happened.

Why did your marriage begin with such promise and deteriorate into such bitterness? Or why has your marriage been so warm and wonderful while your best friend has had nothing but trouble? Why did your neighbor's husband get tired of that role and run away while your spouse has been so faithful? Why did your friend's child experiment with drugs? Why did your neighbor's daughter become sexually active in high school? Why did your friend's son get in trouble with the law? Do you feel helpless when they ask why? They want to know the answers, but you don't have good, foolproof answers to give. There are no packaged answers for life's surprises.

Six weeks before Doug had his fatal accident he was involved in another one. We knew why this one happened. He needed new tires, and he was driving on a rain-slick road. When he put on the brakes, he slid into the intersection. His car was a total loss but his only injury was a substantial bruise on his head. We credited God with saving his life.

But the bruise produced seizures, one at home, one while he was driving the night he died. If we credited God with saving him in the first accident, should we have blamed God for not saving him in the second? Why did God spare him one time but not another? Would you feel helpless to answer these whys?

I have come to believe that *why* may be the unanswerable, and therefore unproductive, question in many of our experiences this side of heaven. Must we know everything? Must we always pry into God's secrets, like an unruly child peeking through a keyhole? Are there not times when it is enough for us to know that God is God? Can't we be content to let God be God in matters beyond human understanding?

I believe that *why* is much less important than *who*. I believe it is much more important to know who will help me out of my hurts than to know who got me into my hurts.

Ultimately we must decide which we trust more—God, or our speculation about God. Our decision rests squarely on the integrity of God's personhood versus the integrity of human speculation about God's personhood. As Abraham said, "Will not the Judge of all the earth do right?" (Gen. 18:25).

Lifechanger 4
Fullness is not always a sign of strength, and emptiness is not always a sign of weakness. To heal your hurts, empty yourself of things that weaken you and fill yourself with things that strengthen you.

Perhaps you have faced the social dilemma I've had at times. The waitress brings a cup of hot coffee to grace the dinner hour, but in my enthusiasm to talk with others at the table, the entire cup grows cold before I begin to drink it. Now what do I do? The waitress comes "to warm up your coffee," but there is no place to put the warm-up. The cup is full, but it is filled with unwanted cold coffee. An asset fifteen minutes ago, a full cup is now a liability. It would be better to have nothing, emptiness, than to have a full cup of cold coffee.

There is only one solution, we must return to the empty cup (waitresses are usually gracious to bring another empty cup) before I can have a full cup again, a full cup of steaming hot coffee.

I have found in this a parallel to life itself. Sometimes my schedule is filled up with cold coffee—small liabilities that fill up the place that significant assets should occupy. Have you ever discovered too late that you have filled your schedule, or your mind, with insignificance so that you have crowded out a rightful place for significance? Or have you found that you have filled your mind with contemporary garbage that crowds out eternal truth? I have, too often! It is easy to allow mediocrity, or even worthlessness, to usurp the rightful place in our hearts where we should instead enthrone truth. It is easy to let a tramp sit on the throne in our hearts where the King should be.

Neither emptiness nor filling in itself is a liability. Neither in itself is an asset. Filling ourselves with the wrong stuff is a personal, and thus a spiritual, liability. Gorging our minds and souls on a sawdust diet of pulp magazines, sleazy novels, and late-night shows but reading little of the Bible and good books is filling ourselves with spiritual emptiness. Emptying our hearts and minds of such things is God's opportunity for filling. Likewise, when our hearts have been drained by woundedness, we may be ripe for God's filling. Thus filling with the wrong thing can be personally emptying and emptying of the wrong thing can be an opportunity for God's filling.

Returning home after Doug's death my heart was empty. It seemed that the cup of life had been tipped over and all its warm, life-giving contents had spilled out. Significance had drained from life's cup, and I stared into the abyss of emptiness.

Emptiness left by death, divorce, debilitating illness, injury, ruptured relationships, job difficulties, and other hurts resembles a black hole that swallows us, sucks us in, but offers no way out, drains the warmth of life from us but offers nothing good in return.

How do I wrestle emptiness? I can wrestle with daily problems and even with principalities and powers (Eph. 6:12), but I can't wrestle a consuming nothingness, a dark void. I don't know how to get hold of it. I reach for something of substance, even unwanted substance, but grasp only my own grasping. How can something that is nothing hold me so tight in its grasp but I cannot grasp it in return?

Several years have passed since that bleak early morning when we flew home to face our family and our emptiness. Since then I have learned that the only antidote to emptiness is filling, not filling up a hole, a place left by a departed loved one, but a filling of the soul with the fullness of God's presence, and that fullness of soul encompasses the dark emptiness, swallows it, if you please.

The psalmist caught the idea when he said, "You . . . anoint my head with oil; my cup overflows" (Ps. 23:5). The anointing oil of the Lord's presence fills the cup drained by these unwanted presences—death, divorce, sickness, broken relationships—and fills it to overflowing. It spills over, flows out, and encompasses the void. The imagery is so much stronger than filling the empty coffee cup. It is an imagery of the extravagance of God's giving of himself, not merely an adequacy to fill up, but a profusion that spills over, a lavish abundance that gushes forth like a fountain, a flood tide of light-giving and life-giving presence, consuming the dark void that tried to swallow me. It is the swallower consuming the swallowed, the greater swallowing the lesser, light swallowing darkness, and thus the light of God's presence becomes a shield between the dark presence and me.

I have learned not to welcome emptiness, any more than I welcome sickness or injury or pain or suffering or any other hurt. But when emptiness seeks to consume me, I welcome the fullness of God's presence, filling up, running over, gushing forth like a fountain. And I learn anew that there is no filling until there is first an emptiness, and I offer my prayer of thanksgiving for the ministry of emptiness that precedes the welcome ministry of God's fullness.

Lifechanger 5
Seeds of strength are planted in the soils of weakness. Your most uplifting strength tomorrow may grow from your most debilitating weakness today.

God made a remarkable statement to the church in prosperous, powerful Corinth, "My power shows up best in weak people" (2 Cor. 12:9 TLB). Paul added an equally remarkable statement, "For Christ's sake, I delight in weaknesses, in insults, in hardships, in persecutions, in difficulties. For when I am weak, then I am strong" (2 Cor. 12:10). At first it would appear that the two verses are saying it is good to be weak so that God will make us strong, which could easily lead us to say "I'm looking for ways to be weak so I can become strong."

If that were true, would I be forced to say, "It's good that Doug was killed so that I can become strong"? Does that mean we should accept each family death or tragedy as cause for celebration because the rest of us will grow stronger? Carried to its extreme, it seems as if we should be glad when a family member is maimed or blinded or killed so that God can do something special for the rest of us. This kind of thinking borders on Darwin's survival of the fittest. The fittest not only survive but are also healthier, wealthier, or wiser because of a family tragedy. I'm sure that isn't what God is saying! It is out of character with other things God has said. No, that can't be it.

Then what is he talking about? How is it that I can be stronger when I become weaker? It's more like the full cup of cold coffee that must be emptied so it can be filled with hot steaming coffee. Self-sufficiency must be emptied so that I can rely upon God's sufficiency.

It's also something like the great tree that grew in the forest. It was magnificent, a royal tree indeed, dominating all the other trees. If this tree could think, and choose, it would of course choose to remain king of the forest. But one day the woodcutters came, laid their axes to this great tree, and cut it down.

The great tree was the picture of weakness and helplessness as it lay on the forest floor. Limbs were cut, and the mighty trunk was severed, cut into pieces, sawed, planed, and sanded, adding to the portrait of weakness and helplessness. At last the great tree was fashioned into elegant furniture to grace the palace. People laughed and made merry as they dined at the table and sat upon the chairs.

Now the great tree was a center of festivities, but it had to be broken first, mutilated, and cut and wounded. No, the tree would not have chosen this humiliation, but having been humiliated it accepted the new glory of gracing the banquet hall of the king.

We do not choose to be wounded, or the manner of our wounding. We do not choose for ourselves or our loved ones to be hurt. But when our lives grace the King's service, somehow we can accept the sawing, hammering, cutting, and sanding that come upon our lives. We may even learn grace to accept these unwelcome refinements cheerfully.

I did not want my son to die. His death hurts, and I am not ashamed to admit the pain, weakness, and helplessness that come from his death. But he did die, and I was helpless to prevent it. There is nothing I can do to reverse his death or stop all the tides of grief and pain that swept over me from his death. But now that I recognize the certainty and the finality of his death, I am anxious that his death will be redemptive, that from his falling to the earth in weakness, like the great tree, something good and strong will come forth to grace the King's service for many years to come.

I think that is what Paul was telling the church at Corinth about God's strength for human weakness: "My strength is made perfect in weakness" (2 Cor. 12:9 KJV). We do not seek weakness, we do not want it, we even shrink from its coming, but when it does come, we allow it to become fertile soil for God's strength to take root. We can even rejoice at such a time, not because tragedy has come but because out of our tragedy can come the springs of redemption.

Have you ever thought of how you would have developed a worldwide, eternal plan of redemption, to be made available to people everywhere? Something that magnificent should command prime-time TV for years to come, neon signs on every mountaintop, the finest public relations agents, the united forces of military might of all superpowers, a union of international banking authorities, in short, every display of power and might that could be mustered.

But God did not do it that way. Instead, when he thought of incarnation, he sent a baby. When he thought of the training of the twelve with whom he would entrust this worldwide mission, he chose fishermen and a tax collector. When he thought of the essence of his plan, atonement, he planned for the death of his only Son. When he thought of the Great Commission, he announced it to a handful of the faithful rather than to the masses. God chose the way of weakness, the path of brokenness, for the grandest display of power the world will ever know. Perhaps you and I can learn something from that.

BROKENNESS

Searching for Order among Life's Shattered Pieces

Dawn announced itself in soft hues as Arlie and I stared through the plane windows. On any other flight we would be chattering about the beautiful colors of the morning sky and basking in the warmth of going home to be with our family.

But this Thursday morning was filled with bittersweet. With the grim news, late last night of Doug's fatal car accident, death's chilling presence had thrust its foot into the doorway of our lives and now threatened to move in and possess the entire house. Since the day each of our five children was born, the small, distant cloud of death hovered over my horizon. It sat there only as a reminder, and a fear, that something could happen to that child.

When Kathy was six I dreamed one night that she had died and was being encased in marble. Waking up that morning was like the resurrection, and all that day I hardly let her out

35

of my sight, smothering her with hugs and kisses. But I quickly
regained my senses and recognized that I could not shadow
her and smother her and still let her grow.

That experience was an early hint of the pulverizing, crush-
ing effect of brokenness. We were to encounter brokenness
again and again during the next three days as we planned for
Doug's funeral and buried his body. We were to know brokenness as we had never known it before.

Arlie and I were anxious to see our children at O'Hare airport, take them into our arms, and pool our helplessness with
theirs. Our family has always been close and it was only right
that we should be together in every facet of this tragedy.

Part of the emptiness of the long night through which we
had agonized was suffering without the rest of the family to
embrace us, and we to embrace them. In this bitter hour it
would be sweet to find comfort in the presence of one another.
Arlie and I had been able to bear the pain of that night because
we had suffered and wept together. We knew also the presence of God that night and knew that the two of us did not
suffer alone. But we needed the others, and it was an aching,
hungry need.

Suffering is always aggravated by loneliness. It is always
more bearable in the presence of those we truly love. I think
that is because the tapestries of love and suffering are often
woven with the same threads.

When we deplaned and saw our children waiting for us, the
sweetness of seeing each face was tempered by the bitterness
of seeing one face missing. Conversely, the bitterness of that
long night in which we became "acquainted with grief" was
tempered by the sweetness of seeing those we loved so much.
As we hugged each one, and wept with each one, the blending of our tears was like the blending of the holy anointing oils

used in Old Testament times, perfumed oils formed from the crushed, broken ingredients, then offered to God. Somehow, I think we all knew that our mingled tears were, like those perfumed oils of ancient times, an offering to God, a plea for his presence more than a bitter lament for Doug's absence.

Together as a family we reluctantly moved into that foreboding world the psalmist described as "the valley of the shadow of death" (Ps. 23:4). We were dragged into that somber world we had never known before, walking among the trappings of death. We had never bought a cemetery plot. Today we must do that. We had never bought a casket or made arrangements for a loved one's funeral. My older brother and sisters had done that for our father and mother. Today we must do those things too.

Arlie and I had not slept throughout the long night, but there was no sleeping now. We had much to do and we would do it together—all of us.

Before plunging into that grim shopping trip, we faced an important decision—could we see Doug, should we see him? His face had been crushed by the accident. Should we see him mutilated? Or should we remember him the way we saw him a week earlier when we hugged him good-bye at the front door. He was living and vibrant then, the Doug we remembered with such delight—hearty laugh, sunny smile, delightful sense of humor, strong handshake, warm embrace. Now we would see a wounded shell, the broken body of the son we had nurtured.

Our children urged us to remember him as he was, rather than carry the vision of a mutilated son through life. We were trying to hear Doug's voice in theirs—would he say this if he were here? I tried to think what I would want if I were to die in a car accident. Would I want my children to remember me

as I was, or have that one last parting moment with my mutilated remains? I thought I would rather have them remember
me as I was instead of as a broken vessel they wouldn't recognize, a fatally wounded father with nothing left but the
shreds of vulnerability.

This was the first of many agonizing choices that day, but
we finally decided not to see him mutilated, to remember him
as a living person. Looking back through the years, I am still
wondering if we made the right decision. Perhaps I should
have seen his crushed body, touched it, and felt the coldness
of death.

As a father, perhaps I should have gazed upon his brokenness. Perhaps I should have participated visually and emo-
tionally in his wounded helplessness. Perhaps I should have
acknowledged my own brokenness in a stark, lonely, empty
moment with his broken body. There is scriptural precedence,
for Jesus asks us to acknowledge our own brokenness at communion as we remember his brokenness. In that way, I participate in his sufferings. Could I have participated more in
Doug's sufferings if I had brought my brokenness before his
broken body? But I didn't.

Now there is forever a comma at the end of Doug's life. I
think I needed a period to punctuate the finality of death,
however painful. I don't know about this for Arlie. A mother's
heart is programmed with a somewhat different software from
a father's heart. Perhaps the decision was right for her but
wrong for me. Perhaps it was wrong for both of us. Or perhaps
we made the right decision after all. Would we have been able
to carry the rest of our lives the image of our son with his skull
crushed in and his face mutilated?

In times of deep hurts you will face similar decisions. Perhaps you have gone through a divorce. Should you throw away

all the mementos and try to erase the memories of better days? Should you try to paint in the minds of your children your ex-mate as villain or should you try to help them understand what you are trying to understand? If you were fired, or forced to resign from your job, should you nurse bitterness against your boss? Or should you look optimistically on the value of the past toward the new opportunities of the future? I can't answer these questions for you, but I urge you to talk them over carefully with God and your most trusted friends and family members before you try to answer them yourselves.

Bob Gray, father of Ron's wife, Becki, and co-pastor of our church, recommended a Christian mortician in Wheaton who became more like a friend than a man in the business of burying the dead. Bob directed our attention to the Wheaton Cemetery, where some of his family and many of our friends were buried. Ironically the cemetery is on the same street, but on the opposite end of town, where I put an engagement ring on Arlie's finger thirty-one years before when we were students at Wheaton College.

Bob also shared a gem of wisdom from his many years as a pastor. "Someone you trust must see Doug, must confirm that it is really him," Bob told me. "Otherwise you will carry a nagging doubt. You will always wonder if you buried someone else." He was so right. I have thought a dozen times since then how wise this counsel was. Then Bob took one more step and became that person. Perhaps I should have gone with him. Or perhaps I should have gone alone. I think I will always be uncertain about that decision.

But you and I must make an important determination now, that decisions made in the past are already made. I really don't know if I made the right decision about seeing Doug. You may be agonizing over actions of the past. Did you make the right choice when you got married? Did you make the right decision when you took the job you have and moved across the country? Did you choose the right career?

I have decided something about my decision, and it may be helpful for you. The decision was made then, and I thought it was right then. No matter what I think now, I can't go back to that point in time and decide again. I must live now with a decision made then, so I must make the most of it. I must look forward, not backward, for that is the direction time moves, and I am caught in the currents of time, swept along by them, and all the wishing in the world will not reverse the movement. All the wishing in the world will not change decisions of the past. If you're like me, you would like to go back and change the really stupid choices you made in the past. But time always looks forward and so must we.

Forgiveness is God's one gracious gift in dealing with our past. Hope for the future is tied inexorably to forgiveness for past mistakes and sins. Forgiveness does not erase the sin, nor does it erase the earthly consequence of that sin, but it does break down the wall of separation between you and the other person and God. Forgiveness reestablishes and revitalizes the person-to-person, one-on-one relationship with the significant others in your life and that is our hope for the future.

Arlie and I had shopped together many times through the years, but always for life-sustaining things—groceries, clothing, gifts, furniture. Each of these had been a stepping-stone toward a more abundant lifestyle, something to enjoy tomorrow, something to make tomorrow a better day. Dark Thursday's shopping trip for a cemetery plot, a funeral, and a casket was a shopping spree in the mall of morbidity. It's hard to think of the resurrection when you are buying a casket. That comes later.

We dealt with "the final resting place," as grave sites are mistakenly called. We arranged final good-byes for a son who had already gone into heaven, beyond the reach of what we would say or buy. It soon became apparent that while this was a tribute to a fallen son, it was in reality shopping for things necessary for us, not for him. At the moment we bought the casket to house his remains, he was already at home in the King's palace. At the moment we bought the grave site where we would lower his body into the ground, he was already ascended into the heavenlies.

No, Doug didn't need these things at all, but we did. It was necessary to buy these things that we really didn't want, but needed, for a son who didn't need them but would probably want us to have them.

These elements in the pageantry of saying good-bye are part of the necessary balm for brokenness. Most of us would not feel good about burying a loved one without them.

Growing up on an Illinois farm, I observed or participated in the disposition of dozens, no hundreds, of dead bodies—chickens, geese, ducks, turkeys, guinea pigs, calves, cows, horses, cats, and a pet dog. With the exception of my pet dog, and perhaps a favorite cat or two, disposition was unceremonious. Smaller animals rated no more than a hole dug in the rich black loam. Larger animals rated the "dead wagon," a truck with a winch that pulled the bloated carcass up a long plank. We were told that the fat from these animals would be used to make soap. It didn't bother us because my mother made our own lye soap, dark yellow chunks that almost took the skin off with the dirt.

But in civilized societies we don't dispose of human bodies that way. Although there are cultural differences, and of course well-known options such as cremation or burial at sea, most people dispose of the bodies of their loved ones with funerals, caskets, graves, and grave markers. These are necessary, not merely as signs of culture, but in respect for the dead, and for the living, putting the period at the end of life's sentence. Those of us left behind need that mark of finality, reminding us one last time that death brings down the curtain on this life's drama and will not raise it again on this earth for anyone (except the few examples in the Bible of people brought back to life).

The Christian distinctive is that God immediately raises that curtain once more in a time transcending time, in a place transcending all geography, in a vitality transcending human limitation, with a personal relationship transcending all defects of personality and faulty relationships. We were assured that while the curtain of Doug's life had closed forever to human sight, it had already been raised beyond mortality, where the mysteries of eternity are revealed at last. While Arlie and I still were seeing God's mysteries "as if we were peering at his reflection in a poor mirror," Doug was already there, where he was now seeing "him in his completeness, face to face" (1 Cor. 13:12 TLB).

We were writing, not the final chapter of Doug's life, for that had been written three nights before, but a postscript, a footnote that said, "Doug, we love you and want to participate in some way in your graduation service into God's eternal home." But it was a post-graduation exercise in which the graduate had already moved on beyond participation. We were engaging in an exercise totally out of keeping with his present condition. The brokenness of the moment was not his, but ours. We were struggling in a pool of broken fragments while he was comprehending eternal wholeness for the first time. We were grieving, not for what he had become, but for

what we would have to become in the interim until we would
join him.

So while Doug basked in eternal sunshine, we sat in the
shadow of death. While he established eternal relationships,
we mourned a broken relationship. While he moved about
the King's palace, we shed our tears in a funeral home, looking at a casket. No, all of this was for us, not for him.

Perhaps that is why we were crying. I know it is, for we were
crying for our own brokenness, while in Doug's new home the
day of his eternal wholeness was dawning. While we mourned
and said good-bye, he was joyfully introducing himself to
God's friends who had crossed the great gulf throughout past
generations. The whole pageantry of death seemed incon-
gruous with eternal life. But the pageant was not for him. It
was for us.

With these things in mind, we planned that the funeral to
be held Saturday would be more a celebration of Doug's life
than a lament for his death. That's what he would have
wanted, we were sure. And that is what we wanted. We knew
that Doug was in the presence of Christ because he had
believed in him and committed his life to him. So it was easier to celebrate life—the life he had when he was with us and
the new life he had already begun in his heavenly home.

This is the kind of funeral I hope my loved ones will prepare when I die. If I have honored God with my life, celebrate!
When you know that I have graduated into God's home, celebrate! While they may feel brokenness in saying good-bye,
the celebration of life will restore a sense of wholeness. That
is what gave us healing when we could have been ground up
in our brokenness.

Not for one minute does that mean our grief is less. Nor
does it mean we are not crushed and broken by this whole

episode. It simply means that in our brokenness and Doug's, which we can't change, we will not submit to death's cold grip; we will not cower under its dark shadow. Instead, we will celebrate life, the life we had and the life we shall have, the life he had with us and the life he has already begun in his final home.

Until the visitation began Friday afternoon, our family was caught up in a maddening whirl of activity, buying what must be bought, arranging the funeral service, making dozens of little decisions. There was no time to ask what had happened and why, no time to ponder, only time to move on an accelerating treadmill racing toward the funeral and burial on Saturday.

Through the years I have always felt deeply pained for those who take one last look at a loved one in the casket, then watch the lid close. How could they bear to see the lid close on someone they love? I had seen my own parents, and Arlie's mother, swallowed into finality this way. It's a grim moment in the pageant of death and burial. With the closing of the lid, the imagery of the great gulf emerges, wider and deeper and more intimidating than the Grand Canyon, separating that person from our touch, our embrace, our words, our care, our gift giving, our laughter, our presence at the dinner table, and separating that person's warmth and presence from us. Never again can we embrace, or be embraced by, that body, watch the sparkle in those eyes, be cheered by the smile on that face, feel the touch from those hands. Never again on this earth can you say the words you really wanted to say but didn't, or withdraw the words you did say but wished you had not. Yes, the lid closing is a grim moment, a sobering experience, but a necessary one to remind us of the finality of death.

For us, there would be no lid closing. The lid was closed in a quiet moment when Arlie and I were not there, with only a stranger to take a last look at him. We never saw him in death. We saw only a casket and were assured he was in it. As painful as it is to watch the lid close, I now think it may have been even more painful to know that we had no option concerning a public viewing. The mortician had told us that he could not repair Doug's face to make it look like him. There could not be an open casket. If we insisted on keeping it open during visitation, we and our friends would look upon the broken face of a stranger and that could leave painful memories. Once again we recognized our helplessness. Even a simple choice like that was not ours to make. It was made for us by circumstance.

TURN YOUR BROKENNESS INTO WHOLENESS

Re-creating the New You

On the second floor of the Wheaton College library stands a large clay pot, excavated from the ancient mound at Dothan, near the place where Joseph was sold into slavery. At first glance the pot appears to be whole, a perfect specimen. But it isn't. Even the slightest second glance shows it to be a whole pot made up of dozens of broken fragments.

The dig at Dothan was conducted many years ago by Joseph Free and his archaeology students. I don't know the specific history of this clay pot, but I know how these things are found and reconstructed.

A dig is a painstaking job, slowly peeling off layer after layer of dirt until an object is found. Before it is removed, it must be carefully recorded as part of that layer. When this pot was found, it was uncovered fragment by fragment, often with a whisk broom. All the fragments were then placed into one container, waiting for a person of enormous patience to restore it.

Then the task of restoring wholeness begins, sorting out the fragments and trying to envision them as a whole pot. It is something like putting together a jigsaw puzzle without any picture on the fragments, nothing but shapes. And not every shape is complete.

At last the pot is assembled, with the fragments glued together so that it is much like the original pot. But of course it is not the original pot. It's different. The original carried water or wine. The reconstructed pot would not hold either. The original was perhaps carried on a donkey or camel, transporting its contents to distant places. The reconstructed pot would not make the trip.

But the reconstructed pot is of much greater value than the original. The original was worth relatively little. It served its purpose when it carried water or wine to a new owner. That's all. The reconstructed pot is an antiquity. The great museums of the world search for pots like these. Restored to their broken wholeness, the pots are treasures of the modern world. Enormous sums of money are spent to find them, restore them, and exhibit them for admiring eyes.

The broken wholeness of the clay pot is a lesson of reconstructed wholeness, increased value, new purpose. We who have been broken by tragedy go through this same cycle—wholeness, brokenness, reconstructed wholeness.

Lifechanger 6
The way to wholeness is through brokenness. When life as you want it to be breaks apart, God can re-create it as he knows it should be.

For several years, when I was a boy growing up on a farm, my mother kept a large glass-topped incubator in a vacant bedroom, with dozens of eggs warmed to the right temperature. We knew the approximate day when I could start watching for the chicks to hatch, and I was always sure to keep an eye on the incubator. I was rewarded with a stunning look at God's cycle of wholeness and brokenness.

At first, the egg was whole. Then at the right time it entered into a state of brokenness. The emergence of new life followed: a baby chick stood there among the broken shells of the egg.

It all started with a small piece of the shell popping off. I could see part of the baby chick in the opening. Then another piece popped off, and another. Before long I could see the chick struggling. All that was within me said, "Open that incubator, help that poor chick go free." But my mother warned me never to do this except in an emergency or I might hurt the baby chick. It was God's master plan for the emerging chick that the egg must go through the process of brokenness, in harmony with the struggles of the chick within. To gain new life, the chick must struggle and the egg must be broken. The destiny of the egg was to be subjected to brokenness in order that new life might emerge. For that purpose the egg came into the world.

I have become increasingly aware since that dark weekend when I buried my son that my wholeness is sustained by brokenness. Without brokenness I cannot have wholeness. Without death I cannot have resurrection, new life. Life, death, life is as much God's established pattern as wholeness, brokenness, wholeness.

My childhood on a grain farm was filled with imagery of wholeness of new life emerging from brokenness. Each spring we plowed the soil; "spring breaking" we called it. Then we pulled a disk over the plowed soil to break it into smaller pieces, and finally we pulled a harrow over it to pulverize it even more. Productivity was directly related to the broken- ness we inflicted on the soil. We had no sympathy for the breaking of the soil, for in its brokenness we found produc- tivity for our crops. No farmer planted his crops without first breaking his soil as much as he could.

Our next step was to plant seed, then hope and pray for that seed to break apart beyond recognition so that a tiny plant could emerge from its heart. From the brokenness of the seed came the new life of the plant that grew into a tall stalk.

Then came harvest. In late autumn, before the winter winds blew, the plant anticipated the brokenness we would inflict upon it and gradually relinquished its greenness, its vibrant life as a plant. With each day of the plant's gradual death, the new grain that grew on it ripened, gradually acquir- ing life-giving properties.

No thoughtful grain farmer would harvest wheat from a vibrant, green plant. It wouldn't grow and it would not make good flour. As the seed died in the spring so that the plant might grow, the plant must die in the autumn so that the seed could gather its life-giving capacity. Only then could it grow a new plant next spring.

At the right time in this cycle of life, we became reapers— cutters, grinders, beaters, and winnowers. Our role as har- vesters was to utterly destroy the plants we had so carefully nurtured throughout the summer months. Is that perhaps why death is sometimes called the grim reaper? The farmer, like death, must do his job so that the transformations in the cycle of life may continue. Without death we cannot be trans- formed from green plants drawing nourishment from earth's soil to another kingdom independent of the soil.

On threshing day we cut the plants, severed them from the sustaining soil where they had grown, and tied them into bundles. With horse drawn hayrack, we gathered the bundles from the field and threw them into an enormous monster called a threshing machine.

It was an awesome sight for a small boy to watch this machine go about its business, the business of inflicting brokenness. Several farmers banded together in those days into threshing rings, moving from one farm to another with this machine to thresh small grain crops such as wheat.

On threshing day a farmer brought his metal monster to our farm, pulled by a giant steam-powered tractor. He unhooked the tractor from the threshing machine, put the two machines face to face, then attached a long belt from a power-driven wheel on the tractor to a matching wheel on the threshing machine.

As the farmer engaged the pulley wheel and coaxed the tractor up to full power, the giant threshing machine came alive, with every belt, wheel, and gear within it joining in a thunderous roar. From the top of the machine came a long pipe, perhaps a foot wide, reaching up, it seemed to me, to the sky. The end of the pipe arched over, presenting an image of a great metal head, pivoting on a long metal neck.

As bundles of grain were tossed into the threshing machine, they were ground into pieces beyond recognition, beaten and flailed. Blowers separated the grain and blew the broken straw from the monster's head, forming enormous strawstacks.

We never felt sorry for the wheat stalks, for we had raised them for this moment of brokenness. All plowing, cultivating, fertilizing, harvesting, and threshing was for one purpose— to extract the life-giving grain from the plants. No, we never mourned this brokenness, for new life came from it. Instead, we sang songs of harvest and felt secure that our grain was safely in before winter.

Sometime before Thanksgiving my father filled a dozen or more sacks with the wheat grain and hauled them to a miller in a neighboring village. The milling machines terrified me almost as much as the threshing machines—chugging, growling, clanking, and wheezing. These machines, like the threshing machines, were instruments of brokenness, but without them the chain of life of the grain would not be completed. At the other end of the machine, the miller gathered buff-colored whole-wheat flour into sacks, which my father hauled back to our farm. Throughout the long winter my mother drew flour from these sacks to make homemade bread. Flour for bread had come through another cycle of brokenness.

But the cycle of brokenness did not end there. It was a special treat to eat a slice of Mom's homemade bread while it was still hot, covered with butter we had churned from pure cream. My teeth ground Mom's masterpiece into unrecognizable bits, and I swallowed it into a long digestive tract where it would be broken again and again until it could be absorbed into my bloodstream, permitting this growing boy to be nourished and kept alive.

I am alive today because I submitted myself to these cycles of brokenness, year after year, day after day. The farmer who feels sorry for his soil and refuses to break it will die. The harvester who feels sorry for his crops and refuses to break the plants he nurtured will die. The miller who feels sorry for the grain and refuses to grind it into flour will die. And the boy who feels sorry for his mother's loaf of bread and refuses to grind it into pieces with his teeth will not grow to become a man.

Why did God choose brokenness as the essential element of growth, and health, and life? Or to put it another way, why did God choose brokenness as the necessary prelude to wholeness? He could have chosen another system, of course, because he is God. But he didn't. He chose brokenness to bring wholeness to life. Perhaps it is because brokenness is a freeing process.

The nutrients of the soil are freed most when the soil is broken, the wheat plants yield their grain best when they are cut and mutilated, the wheat grain yields flour most when crushed, and my mother's bread gives up its nourishment most when ground and digested into the smallest particles imaginable.

Could it be that the process we fear most, to be broken, is the very process that frees us to be what we should ultimately become? Could it be that our natural tendency to preserve our wholeness, resist brokenness, is antithetical to God's established plan for us? Could it be that we, like a grain of wheat, must be broken to free our life-giving gifts to those around us?

I don't like to be broken any more than you. But when I am broken, I want God to release life-giving gifts for the healing of other broken people around me. As Jesus said, "Unless a kernel of wheat falls to the ground and dies, it remains only a single seed. But if it dies, it produces many seeds" (John 12:24).

Lifechanger 7
Beauty and fragrance are released through brokenness. When you are broken, ask how you can grace the life of someone else through this experience.

In the Nazareth synagogue one day Jesus read from Isaiah 61, a chapter filled with images of brokenness—poverty, brokenheartedness, imprisonment, captivity, mourning, despair, devastation, and ruin. With those images most of us would associate defeat, failure, despair, and depression.

But Isaiah didn't. Instead, he spoke of good news, freedom, release, the Lord's favor, comfort, beauty, gladness, praise, renewal, and restoration. He even said a crown of beauty would come from ashes and oil of gladness would come from mourning. At first glance, it doesn't make sense. Anyone knows that beauty comes from health and prosperity, not from the ashes of defeat, and gladness comes from vitality and success, not from mourning.

Why would we ever expect fragrance from brokenness? It isn't natural. It isn't normal. Brokenness should produce a stench, a raw putrid smell that turns others away. Why the difference?

The difference is Jesus. He said that the prophecy in Isaiah 61 was about himself, and that it was fulfilled that day in Nazareth (and today wherever you are). Jesus presides over the life cycle in which we are so much involved, for he is Life. "I am the way and the truth and the life," he said (John 14:6).

Isaiah listed all the broken pieces of life without Jesus—poverty, brokenheartedness, despair, devastation, and ruin. By ourselves we see nothing but the ashes, the rottenness, the decay, the hopelessness. We cannot see life beyond the rotting seed or life beyond the dying plant. It took the creative genius of God to see a green plant in a rotting seed, a rich grain of wheat in a dying stalk, bread in the hard kernel of wheat, and a growing boy or girl in a loaf of bread. It also took the creative genius of God to see John Bunyan in prison and envision *Pilgrim's Progress*. That's why Isaiah listed in the same chapter the attributes of wholeness re-created from the fragments of brokenness—good news, freedom, release, the Lord's favor, comfort, beauty, gladness, praise, renewal, and restoration.

With Jesus the ashes of brokenness can become a crown of beauty and the sting of mourning can become oil of gladness.

Why? How? It sounds flippant merely to say that Jesus makes the difference. I want to know how he makes that difference.

Last Sunday we served communion in our church. As I drank the tiny cup of grape juice and ate the scrap of bread, I reflected back to that afternoon almost two millennia ago when Jesus died. Then I remembered what Isaiah said about the crucifixion, writing nine hundred years before it happened. "He was wounded for our transgressions, he was bruised for our iniquities: the chastisement of our peace was upon him; and with his stripes we are healed" (Isa. 53:5 KJV). I marveled as I reflected on these words.

When Doug died, I was wounded. To be Christlike, I must help make his wounds and mine *for* something. When our wheat seed died under our soil, it died *for* the plant that was emerging. When our wheat plant died and was cut and broken into a hundred pieces, its brokenness was *for* the seed that was ready to harvest. The seed died for the plant and the plant died for the seed, and year after year this self-sacrificing cycle continued. A selfish seed or a selfish plant that refused to die would end the cycle of life.

This, of course, is what the cross is all about. We speak of redemption. We talk about atonement. That's another way of saying Jesus' crucifixion was *for* something, for someone—for me, for you, for the person still rejecting him, for the healing of the nations. A selfish Savior would have terminated God's grand design for redemption.

One day Jesus was a dinner guest at the home of a man known as Simon the leper. Simon was probably one of the many lepers Jesus healed, and the grateful man invited him to dinner. While Jesus was reclining at Simon's table, as people did in those days, a woman came with an alabaster jar filled with a very expensive scented oil, made of pure spikenard. As long as the jar was whole and sealed tightly, the fragrance was contained, and thus would not serve its purpose.

But when the woman broke the jar, she freed the spikenard to do what it was intended to do, to offer its fragrance to all who were there. The woman did this as an act of love, an early anointing of Jesus for his death. But it was actually a symbol of the fragrance released by the broken, bruised Jesus on the cross.

I have heard that certain spices release their fragrance or flavor only when crushed. Whole pepper, for example, releases its flavor for your dinner when you grind it. Many spices are like that, aren't they? Most spices in your spice rack are ground into powder. Flavor or fragrance is there, but brokenness releases it.

Now I think I have discovered something. Wounding, hurts, mourning can easily lead to despair or depression. But on the other hand, they can also lead to healing. Woundedness or brokenness can leave us limp and lifeless, crying for ourselves and our unwanted circumstances. Or we can let woundedness and brokenness release our own inner beauty and fragrance, but even more the greater beauty and fragrance in us for the healing of those we touch. The margin of difference for me is the degree to which I allow Jesus to be my Life, in me and through me.

If I were planning a grand scheme of redemption for the world, I would not focus it on the death of my son. I would muster all the power and might that I could and dazzle the world with my plan. But God chose another way, the way of brokenness, because he knew something that I am gradually discovering, that brokenness is his way toward wholeness. He knew that the alabaster jar of my life must be broken for the fragrance to be released. But of course I must let it be released.

God in Christ is not asking us to do what he is unwilling to do. He is not a spectator in the arena of brokenness, but a participant. This is what I learn from Isaiah 53. He was wounded (broken) for our transgressions, bruised (broken) for our iniquities, chastised (broken) so that we may have peace. His woundedness, or brokenness, was for someone, for me, for my cycle of life, and Doug's cycle of life, to continue beyond the final curtain call on this earth.

5

SEPARATION

Standing at the Edge of the Great Divide

Heavy rains swept through Illinois the night before Doug's funeral, and with the gray rain-streaked dawn came a new concern. We had been preoccupied with the trauma of burying our son, and now came the nightmarish worry of burial in mud and driving rain. Nothing is so bad but what it can become worse, and now it seemed that the worst had come. Throughout my lifetime I have attended many funerals and have conducted several. Some of these funerals took place in snow or rain, but the rain was always a light drizzle, like a scene from a black and white movie set in old England. Never had I seen a funeral in driving rain with oversaturated ground. Now I might see it for the first time at the funeral of my own son.

The service began in our church at 10:00 A.M. and with it a fresh wave of rainstorms, this time accented with lightning and thunder. The rain pounded on the church roof with a staccato beat, punctuating my growing concern for the burial at the cemetery. Wasn't it agony enough to bury our son today? Why the added agony of burying him in the mud and driving rain?

Two nights earlier, on Thursday, we had planned the funeral service. Some decisions were simple, such as involving our co-pastors, Bob Gray and Jay Kesler, in the service. Doug's cousin Tim Allen and his wife, Jane, are outstanding vocalists, so we wanted them to sing. Another cousin, Dave Masterson, is an accomplished pianist and his wife, Marie, a talented violinist, so we wanted them to play. But what would be the opening hymn? Of all hymns, what would best express what we wanted to say at such a time as this?

Little did we realize then how much music at a funeral or wedding can impact us for years to come. We chose the stately hymn, "Guide Me, O Thou Great Jehovah" to open the service because it captured something of the Lord's majesty as a focus of our celebration of life. It is a song of Jehovah's mighty guidance for the weak pilgrim, his healing waters on life's journey, his safe passage across the Jordan into the Promised Land, and the dispelling of fear and doubt because of his presence. The refrain, "songs of praises, songs of praises, I will ever give to Thee," reaffirmed our commitment to praise God, even in this most difficult hour. Ever since that Saturday morning, whenever we sing this hymn, Arlie and I instinctively reach for each other's hand and we sense our own personal need for our Great Jehovah to lead us through the pilgrim land in which we walk.

"Finally Home," a duet Tim and Jane sang, has the same impact on us. Almost four years later, as I was driving home from Wheaton one afternoon, I saw in my rearview mirror a beige Volkswagen Rabbit approaching. It was identical to the car Doug drove when he died. I stared in disbelief at the driver, who in the rearview mirror could have passed for Doug's identical twin, or Doug himself! The combination of these two visual images had an electric effect on me. I was stunned! Was I imagining things? I looked again. Yes, it was there and the young man was there and he looked like Doug. Before I could recover from the shock, someone on the radio began to sing "Finally Home." I am still stunned by the combination of these three.

The music we choose to grace our uniting or our separation will linger with us for a lifetime, opening floodgates of memories for good or evil for years to come. I wonder how many people have reconsidered divorce after listening together to their wedding music. If you are having marital hurts, you may want to play your wedding tape, if you have one, or play "your song," a special song with meaning for both of you when times were better. It won't resolve your problems, but it may create a more sensitive climate in which you can work them out.

I had thought once of giving the memorial message, but I didn't think I could do it. Things had happened too fast. I was still in shock. I remembered how much I admired my friend Joe Bayly when he gave the memorial message for his son Joe Jr. I had just hired Joe at the publishing company where I worked when his son was involved in a tragic accident. The family had not yet moved from the Philadelphia area, so I went there to be with Joe and Marylou. It was not I who ministered to them, but they who ministered to me. It takes a very strong father to do what Joe did, and I wasn't sure I was that strong.

By the close of the service the rain had stopped. There would be a luncheon buffet in the fellowship hall and after that the burial. I hoped and prayed that the rain was indeed over so we would be spared the added agony.

Like closing the lid on the casket, the graveside service emphasizes the finality of death, bringing down the curtain on the drama of earthly existence, the termination of the sight, sound, and touch of a person we know and love. Never again can we hug or kiss or touch or share a good meal with this person. Never again can we talk with him, joke with him, think with him, plan with him. Never.

I remember little of the service itself. We gathered some of the beautiful flowers to put in our home as a memorial to Doug for those who would come there. Some we left at the grave as a loving tribute to Doug, and a reminder that life, like flowers, can fade quickly.

The one memory of that day etched deep in my mind, a memory that will not go away, is the sight of Arlie, lingering for one last look at the casket, softly whispering, "Good-bye, Doug." This was the son she had carried through nine months of pregnancy, the child she had nursed, fed, and bathed. She had changed a thousand diapers for him, read to him, listened to him, counseled him, coaxed him to practice for music lessons, chauffeured him, attended his recitals and orchestra concerts and Little League games, and hundreds of other things a busy mother does without complaint.

Of all the hurts on that day, I believe that was the most painful, because in those simple words, "Good-bye, Doug," all of the pain of separation is summarized. Those simple words remind us of the great gulf, the enormous divide, between the living and the dead. There is a one-way path stretching across that gulf. Each of us will walk across one way. But no one returns and that is what makes separation such a harsh reality.

Separation from my son stirred me to wonder about my hurts and how I might be healed, and how I might help others be healed from their hurts too. I discovered that the world around me is filled with hurting people, and they are hurting because something in their wholeness as a person has been damaged or destroyed.

It is this realization of damaged wholeness that forces us to take a new look at personhood. Before we understand why we hurt, we must understand how we are whole.

TURN YOUR
SEPARATION
INTO REACHING OUT

Bringing Life Together
by Embracing Others

The story of the early church is one of triumph and tragedy. With the coming of the Holy Spirit, the church exploded with growth. Thousands became believers, almost overnight. The early believers were at the pinnacle of success. Where would it all end?

Then tragedy struck. Persecution began. Believers in Jerusalem were threatened. They had to move away to save their lives. Separated from home and family, these early believers must have thought their new-found success had come to an end.

But this was God's plan, a plan for new beginnings. He knew that this body of believers would build a fence around them-

selves in Jerusalem. They would become ingrown. Of course this
could not happen. The gospel was for the whole world, and God
must see that his people went out to the whole world with it.

Comfortable people riding high on success don't often leave
home to take their message to new places. No, these people
had to be separated from home and family and comfort and
success. That was the only way they would reach out to a needy
and hungry world, waiting to hear their gospel message.

It may take separation, a tragedy, in our lives to make us
reach out too.

Lifechanger 8
*Losing someone important makes you
reevaluate yourself and your purpose.
Healing the hurt of separation comes, not
by dwelling on what you have lost, but by
helping God revitalize who you are
and what you can do.*

What hurts about losing Doug is not only that I lost a son,
but that I lost an important part of myself. Doug was his own
person, to be sure, an individual with a mind of his own and
a life of his own and we were careful not to intrude into his
privacy. But sonship never stands completely independent of
fatherhood or motherhood.

Before I married Arlie, each decision was based on what I
wanted to do. But when I married her *I* became *we*. For all but
very personal decisions I stopped asking, "What should I do?"
and began asking, "What should we do?"

Then we had children, five of them. *We* took on new meaning and became a widening circle. When we planned a vacation,
the children were important to that decision. When we thought

about career, and home, and activities, and church, and a hundred other things, we always embraced the seven of us.

My wife and children are "significant others," those who are essential to my wholeness as a person. Without them I am an incomplete person, not because it was essential for me to marry and have five children, but because now that we are part of one another's wholeness, all of us are *we* to each of us.

Draw a circle. Within it draw three small circles about one third of the larger one. Write ME in one, SIGNIFICANT OTHERS in another, and GOD in the other. That's what I think is really me, the whole me. When I became a Christian, I asked God to live in me and through me. God is an essential part of my wholeness. When I profess to be a Christian, I am not even a whole person if God does not live in me and through me. When I embrace significant others, they are part of my wholeness, part of the whole me.

God and significant others are not compartments or divisions of my wholeness. They are part of my *undivided* wholeness.

The significant others in the second circle include my wife and children, my career as a writer and editor, my church, and my close friends. Sever one of these from me and you remove part of me, a part of my *undivided* wholeness.

So you are more than yourself, and I am more than myself. When you understand that, you will understand why you hurt so much when you lose a significant other, someone who has been a significant part of you.

After twenty years of marriage, a friend I will call Roberta learned for the first time that her husband was a practicing homosexual. For several years he had been secretly meeting other men in a nearby city. When Roberta discovered that, she lost her husband and her marriage, of course. But since a husband is a significant other, especially after twenty years of marriage, she lost part of herself, not merely one compartment labeled *husband*, but a part of her undivided whole person.

This is the stuff from which damaged self-esteem is made. When a significant part of your undivided wholeness is damaged, your self-esteem is damaged. Fortunately, Roberta was a mature Christian and was wise enough to ask what she had to do to turn her hurts into healing. Before long she was helping other damaged wives. In turning others' hurts into healing, her own pain was relieved. Today she has a significant ministry with other women.

Let me illustrate undivided wholeness this way. You inherit a hundred-acre farm from your father, who inherited it from his father and so on for several generations. It has family value in addition to intrinsic value and productive value, so you prize the farm. But to borrow money for a business deal, you mortgage the farm. The bank now has a mortgage for 25 percent of the total value of your farm. Your business deal goes sour and you can't pay the bank, so the bank is willing to settle for 25 percent of your farm. You want to let the bank take 25 acres to settle the debt, but the bank doesn't want to be in the business of farming. You discover that the mortgage makes provision for the bank to take 25 percent of the undivided whole. That means the bank now owns, not 25 acres, but 25 percent of your 100 acres, the same 100 acres of which you own 75 percent. Like it or not, you have lost part of all your farm (rather than all of part of your farm).

And like it or not, when you lose a significant other in your life, you lose a part of all of you, not merely a part of you. That's why divorce or spouse abuse or child abuse or the loss of an important job or a hundred other losses of significant others can be so devastating. You do not merely lose a job or dignity or income or whatever else you think you lost. You lose an undivided part of your personal wholeness.

Lifechanger 9
The pain of separation may come from your own self-imposed isolation. Turn your hurt of separation into healing by reaching out to someone who needs your loving interest and concern.

Many years ago I attended a small worship service in another city and was asked not to take part in communion. Since communion was the focal point of the service, I was really asked not to participate with them in their worship. My sin? I was studying for the ministry, and these people believed Christians should gather without ministers, so I was rejected, excluded, if you please, from their concept of wholeness as a body of believers. I don't want to criticize these people because they appeared to be very devout Christians and earnest Bible students. But their sense of wholeness as a body of believers was rigidly exclusive, so exclusive that they wanted no part of a minister. I was tainted, and they would not be corrupted by a minister in their midst.

Before we become too critical of this thinking, we should consider who we reach out to help and to heal. Do we put our arms around a person of another race to help him or her as brother or sister? What about a divorced person? A battered wife? A former prostitute who has become a new Christian? A man who has served time in prison and has become a Christian there? The list is endless, isn't it?

Being separated from Doug has led me to ponder the price tag on personhood, God's price tag. It has led me to ask what value God assigns to those we so easily reject, some who are true believers already and some who need our loving involvement to help them become true believers. Death, divorce, or any one of a dozen other losses separates us from another person even when we choose not to be separated. But exclusivity deliberately separates us from another person, creating a form of death in which a gulf is placed between us.

I am very much aware that a local church fellowship is a voluntary gathering of persons who have much in common, desire one another's company, desire to unite in Christian service. Churches thrive when there is a common bond for fellowship, and not when we force-feed fellowship.

I was rejected by my brothers and sisters in the exclusive group, not because I was personally incompatible with their fellowship, but because they viewed the body of Christ as their exclusive body, and those outside their specific body were therefore dead to Christ's body. They knew I had no desire to crash the party and become part of their continuing fellowship because I lived 150 miles away. I wanted only to share the Lord's Table with the Lord's people because I assumed they and I were all members of the body of Christ.

If they had said to me, "We know you are a Christian and you're welcome to share communion with us, but we prefer that you not join our church; you just don't fit our group," I really could understand that. Instead, they were saying, "You can't share communion with us, so we don't recognize you as part of the body of Christ, the same body of which we are a part." Wholeness in Christ accepts Christ's people as His body. It is not exclusivity.

We have built so many walls to fence us in and fence others out—denominational walls, walls of doctrinal fine tuning, cultural walls, exegetical walls, and so on. Jesus said that he "came to seek and to save what was lost" (Luke 19:10). We who follow him should do no less. Wholeness in Christ is reaching out to the whole body of Christ in fellowship and to those outside the body of Christ in winsomeness to bring them his healing.

Wholeness is not completeness. My life is still under construction. I hope it is more finished than a new believer's life. If it isn't, my last four decades of Bible study and Christian activity have been wasted. But my life is still being hammered, chiseled, sanded, and polished in the hands of the Master Carpenter.

To be a whole person is to be what God wants me to be today. I may be challenged to new heights of wholeness tomorrow. Roberta, who discovered her husband was a homosexual, was challenged that way. She was a whole Christian before she learned of her husband's waywardness. But her discovery brought her to a fork in the road. She would either go down to utter defeat, succumb to her brokenness, lie shattered in pieces in the pit, and wallow in her own self-pity, or she would rise to serve, and in serving hurting people find healing for her own wounds.

You and I will never be complete persons this side of heaven. Our lives should always be under construction, always seeking God's refinement. But we can be whole in Christ.

Lifechanger 10
Healing comes, not by how well you avoid all loss, but by how you respond to loss when it comes. Hurt comes whether or not you choose it, but healing comes only because you choose it.

When our son died, I joined a new fellowship filled with the ranks of hurting people. I never realized before how many hurting people surround me. Hurts and suffering are not exclusive; they embrace us all, and come in a full assortment.

Twice during the past year as I planned for this book I clipped every newspaper article I could find where someone was hurt. I did this for a week last spring and another week last fall. You could anticipate many common hurts—murder, rape, accidents from drunken driving, drug abuse, divorce, separation, and job loss. Each week I found about forty different kinds of hurts.

There was a man who ridiculed his wife for being fat. When she lost weight he accused her of cheating on him. One man lost vast sums of money on Black Monday and shot his stockbroker. A twelve-year-old boy raped a four-year-old girl, following instructions from a dial-a-porn call; an eighteen-month-old girl fell into an abandoned well and was rescued after workers drilled two and a half days through solid rock to reach her; biological parents with second thoughts about giving their child for adoption were arrested for kidnapping the child from the adoptive parents. The list is endless.

Several adults we know had painful childhoods. Some were abused, some were neglected, some were made to feel inferior, some were treated as nonpersons, some had parents who built their own self-esteem by destroying the child's self-esteem, making themselves look good, they thought, by making their child look bad. There is nothing these persons can do to erase what happened. Not one of them can go back and change what was. In that sense, the past is past. If you have been wounded through a painful childhood, the first step on the road to healing is to recognize that you can't change what happened then.

You are likely carrying some personal hurt. Most of us do. That hurt can continue to eat away at your personhood, like a cancer, spreading across your emotions and spirit. When this happens, the spreading malignancy will damage you and your self-esteem.

The damage comes, not merely because you are separated from someone or something important to you, but because you are separated from something that became a significant part of you. You are suffering from a breach of wholeness. An undivided part of you as a whole person is separated from you. No wonder self-esteem suffers.

Nothing you think or do will erase what happened in the past. You may not even change the minds of the people who inflicted hurts on you. But you can change yourself. You can turn your hurts into healing by the way you respond. You may have no choice concerning your pain. But you do have a choice concerning the way you respond to it. Here are five options:

Self-pity

It's easy for us to feel sorry for ourselves. "It's not fair!" we said when we were children. That's true! Life isn't fair. Some of the nicest people I know have been burned by circumstances beyond their control. It's not fair. It really isn't. Bullies do win, nice guys do finish last, downtrodden people do get kicked in the face when they are down. Failure seldom visits us with one knockout blow but usually comes with a one-two-three punch, hitting us again and again.

A baby is born with a handicap. Perhaps it is a physical defect that limits his activity. Or perhaps he was born with a learning disability. Or his family is poor, or his father can't keep a job, or his mother is an alcoholic or a slovenly housekeeper. It could be any of a hundred handicaps that separate him from his peers. It isn't his fault, and it may not be his parents' fault. Perhaps it was no one's fault. But it's there.

The boy doesn't do well in school, so he feels inferior to his classmates. He isn't chosen for teams, even for casual games on the playground, so he feels inferior to his playmates. His "friends" may tease him and call him cruel names. At home, a thoughtless parent may casually compare him to his brother or sister. "Why can't you do what they do?" is the implication. "Why can't you be like them?"

How can a child develop positive self-esteem when everyone is pushing him down and kicking him in the face? It isn't fair. It really isn't.

This handicapped boy can't change his handicap. He can't change his parentage, his father's career, his mother's alcoholism, his learning disability, or his limp. As a boy, he may not be able to understand what is happening or what he should do about it. As a rejected boy, he may not be able to do anything except dig his pit a little deeper each day. But along the road to manhood, someday he will face a decision, or many decisions, that will determine how he responds to his hurt.

At some point you and I and everyone we know must make a conscious decision about our hurts and how we will respond. To phrase it in computer language, our default drive takes us automatically to self-pity, it is the response we make unless we send an alternative signal to ourselves.

Self-pity is celebration standing on its head. It is lament, a negative tribute to our wound. In biblical times people often put on sackcloth and ashes as a public lament, public mourning, for their misfortunes. They could have gone into the privacy of their home to mourn. Instead they displayed it. We must not criticize them, for our funerals are our sackcloth and ashes. And our natural inclination when we are wounded is toward self-pity.

Self-pity robes self in sackcloth and ashes and laments self to another public—self. It is self lamenting self before self. Self seeks stroking from its audience (self) for its own wounds (separation of one part of the undivided wholeness of self from another). Self-pity seeks to make us feel good about feeling bad. It seeks to make wretchedness its own reward. Self-pity is a consolation prize, a medal bestowed on self for a breach in selfhood. It is therefore an exercise in futility, like the dog chasing its own tail and then rewarding itself with a bone as a consolation prize for not catching it.

Self-pity lets us wallow in our misfortunes so they stroke us and soothe us. It doesn't change our hurts and it doesn't change us, but it just rewards us with fool's gold feelings.

Self-pity also demands stroking from others. Since I feel so bad, why don't you feel that way too? Self-pity has no therapy for wounds, no healing for others through your woundedness. It is false security concerning insecurity. Don't encourage it. It has nothing to offer you.

Self-pity sends out signals, good and bad, to attract the attention of self. Self-pity asks self to come and mourn for self. Self begs self to bestow medals of honor for wounds received in life's combat. It is divisive, for it asks the whole me to divide myself so that one part of me can mourn for the other part of me. In that sense, it also asks one part of me to bring glory to the other part of me. Since no one else understands my hurt, I will ask myself to understand it and award myself in recognition of my hurt. Self must come and pay tribute to self, not for achievement, but for hurts.

Jesus spoke clearly about matters of the heart. He spoke in this passage about fasting, but I think it applies equally for self-pity. In both situations the person is asking reward for hurts or deprivation of the heart. Jesus said, "When you fast [or when you hurt], do not look somber . . . But . . . put oil on your head and wash your face, so that it will not be obvious to men that you are fasting, but only to your Father, who is unseen; and your Father, who sees what is done in secret, will reward you" (Matt. 6:16–18).

Jesus is telling us that secret matters are between us and God. They are not to be displayed before others (including self) for pity or reward. God alone should reward or punish us for matters of the heart. Public conduct is another matter.

Self-depreciation

Deep wounds, such as the loss of a loved one, leave scars on our personhood. The night we heard of Doug's fatal car accident we slowly began to realize that we would be different persons from that time on. The question is not will we be different after we are deeply wounded, but how will we be different?

Since Doug was one of the significant others in my life, he was part of me, part of my personhood. I lost a son, but I also lost part of my undivided wholeness. If I had assigned my son to one compartment of my personhood, if I had established sonship and fatherhood with fences around each so that the one coudn't spill into the other, if I had never made the transition from I-ness and you-ness to we-ness, I would not have lost part of my undivided wholeness that night. But I also would have been a very selfish, self-centered person.

When we lose part of our undivided wholeness, we tend to lose self-esteem. When we lose that, we put a lower price tag on ourselves than before. Esteem is not pride unless it is inflated. Esteem is the value we place on our personhood. If the price tag is exaggerated, we have sunk into pride. If it is undervalued, we have sunk into self-depreciation, low self-esteem. Self-depreciation also comes from perfectionism, estimating what you ought to do much higher than what you can do or even should do.

It's easy to lose self-esteem and thus depreciate yourself when you have lost part of your undivided wholeness. It's natural when you have lost a significant part of yourself to think of yourself as less valuable than before.

But losing undivided wholeness does not mean you are worth less any more than losing that extra fifty pounds of weight throughout your body. We change. But we are not less. We are different. But we are not deficient. Losing Doug changed me, for I lost a significant part of my undivided wholeness. But with what is left, I can commit myself to being an even more effective healer of damaged persons. I must not think more or less of myself, but recognize only that God may use me more effectively.

Revenge

The bumper sticker on the car ahead of me, pasted on the trunk, read, RESERVED SEAT FOR EX-HUSBAND. It could have been pasted on the woman's doghouse too. There was a slight thirst for revenge in her sentiment, a desire to get even.

We have all wanted to get even with someone for some wrong done to us. But there really is no such thing as getting even. How can you hope to measure evenness in wrongdoing?

Let's say Molly's husband has an affair with his secretary. What should Molly do, what could Molly do to get even? If Molly had an affair with her neighbor, would that even the score? Not really, because two wrongs do not equalize one wrong. Also two more people are involved now, the neighbor and his wife. Now the neighbor's wife may want to get even, with her husband and with Molly. So what does she do to equalize things?

So how else could Molly get even? What if she demanded the mink coat she had always wanted? Or what if she demanded a new sports car? Molly will have a new coat or a new sports car, but she will still have memories of the affair. Her husband can't buy back her good graces or affection.

Molly could punish her husband, deny him sex for a year, or two years, or forever. She could stop talking to him or remind him every day how wretchedly angry she is at him. She could demand that they separate and live in two different places. Or she could get a divorce.

These are all options that Molly will likely consider, but not one of them gets even. The truth is, there is no way to get even for wrongdoing. Even if Molly devised a clever way to get revenge, how will she know when the revenge equals the sin? How can it ever exactly equal the sin?

If Molly's revenge equals more than the sin, does her husband have the right to sin a little more to even things out? A marriage like that isn't much of a marriage, is it?

Revenge is not a good option in solving conflict because it creates a pendulum effect, with each swing of the pendulum, each attempt to get even, escalating the conflict. The entire Middle East conflict could be solved if the element of revenge was removed. But it will not be solved because revenge continues and revenge always pays back a little more rather than getting even. Then the other side must pay back a little more and the conflict continues to escalate.

God has the answer to revenge, "Do not take revenge . . . for it is written, 'It is mine to avenge; I will repay' says the Lord. On the contrary, 'If your enemy is hungry, feed him; if he is thirsty, give him something to drink. In doing this, you will heap burning coals on his head.' Do not be overcome by evil, but overcome evil with good" (Rom. 12:19–21). God is telling us, don't try to get even, but let the other person get more than you.

Forgiveness

In his Sermon on the Mount, Jesus gave the only workable alternative to revenge and getting even—forgiveness. Then he practiced on the cross what he preached on the mountain.

The Scriptures are filled with rich imagery concerning forgiveness. At one time it means to cancel a debt, at another time to release someone from an obligation. At one time it suggests covering a sin so that it is obscured, at another time it portrays the giving of a remarkable gift with unconditional favor. In the Old Testament there is a close association between forgiveness and atoning sacrifices.

Atonement, "at-one-ment," paints a picture of restoration, putting broken pieces together again, bringing together two persons who were separated or estranged. The atoning sacrifices in the ancient offerings were to restore people estranged from God back into fellowship with him.

An atoning sacrifice is the offering of value necessary to restore separated people. Jesus' death on the cross was the offering of highest value (God's Son) to reconcile us to God.

Is it possible that more marriages might be saved through atoning sacrifices, at-one-ment sacrifices? Is it possible that more friendships might be restored, more parent-child relationships might be salvaged, more hurt feelings might be absolved with an at-one-ment sacrifice?

God's forgiveness absolves the sinner from his sin, releases him from the penalty he deserves because of his sin. Our forgiveness does not carry that weight. Only God can forgive sin and release someone from its penalty. Our forgiveness releases us from the anger, bitterness, desire for revenge, and voluntary estrangement from the one who sinned against us. It releases us from the demand we would make for getting even.

Let's look again at the man who had an affair with his secretary. After great agony and soul searching, and after the husband repented and showed an earnest desire to be reconciled with his wife, she said, "I forgive you." Did she forgive his sin? Not really. He will have to ask God to do that. No wife on earth can do that. Did she absolve him from all consequences of his act? No, because the secretary's husband may still plan to get even and may still cause trouble for the man. The man's wife can't do much about that. Her forgiveness doesn't cover the secretary's husband. Her forgiveness simply says to her husband, "I will no longer try to get revenge. I will not try to get even. I release you from my anger and bitterness and estrangement and desire for revenge. I release you from all the penalty I wanted to send upon you. My slate where all your wrongs were written is clean."

This is the basis for at-one-ness. If the man truly repented and the woman truly forgave, they can be at one again. Reconciliation, atonement, is that way with God too, isn't it?

Redemption

There is one step even more noble, more productive, more elevating, more wonderful than forgiveness: at-one-ness. This plan is uniquely God's plan, a plan to make castles from ashes, silk purses from sows' ears, prophets and apostles from ordinary fishermen, preachers and missionaries from vile slave traders, God's ambassadors from common criminals. His plan is simply known as redemption, making something of great worth from worthlessness.

Later we will talk much more about redemption, so it is enough here to list it as an option in responding to your hurts. Take a new look at yourself and see what you can become, even as a wounded person, in the hands of the Creator.

LONELINESS

Learning to Live with Absence

Like most funerals, Doug's ended with friends surrounding us with loving arms at home. We ate, sang, prayed, and talked. Anyone who has lost a loved one knows how important these baptisms of love are to the survivors immediately after the funeral. But if you are a survivor, you also know how lonely life gets when everyone leaves.

I have ached many times for men or women who lose their mate, find themselves surrounded, almost smothered, with love from hundreds of people who embrace them and offer the few words they can say at such a time, then face that overpowering aloneness when everyone leaves.

Fortunately people leave us gradually, so withdrawal into loneliness is not abrupt. Acquaintances usually go first, then close friends and family members, who usually linger as long as they can.

I have often thought that it would be better if we could reverse the order in funerals. Invite friends and family members in before the deceased is gone and let him or her enjoy the party. But how do we know when our time is coming, and if we do, we probably will not feel like a big party with hundreds of friends around us. It might be a bit awkward to get excited about our own funeral. It would certainly be a downer to see everyone go and realize that we too must leave—alone. No, we must keep the system we have. It is not a pleasant system, but I really can't think of a better one.

The time came when our friends had to leave. They, too, had homes and families. Then our married children, Brad and Kathy, and Ron and Becki, had to leave, for they also had their own homes. Two days later Jan had to return to college and Cindy had to get back to classes at high school. We were so grateful for the evenings, when Cindy could be home.

But during the day life settled down to Arlie and me alone. Days were different now, for Doug had been living at home while he began his career and completed graduate school.

The darkroom where Doug did many hours of photographic work was near my study downstairs. Whenever he had come down, several times a day, he lit up his infectious smile and waved to me. Often he would stop to chat. How many times after the funeral I would look up and expect him to be there waving. But of course he wasn't. I knew that was a vanished reality, an image only in my mind. In the absence of the living person, we cling to images of the past, projecting them into a present circumstance, a faint wisp of what was. These images from the past, projected onto the screen of the present, bring with them a deep sense of loneliness. I began to realize that we would be lonely, not only for Doug, but for all the pleasant sights and sounds associated with him. We longed for Doug, but we also longed for all the excitement and delights that came with him.

You may find in your own situation a blur between the loneliness for the person and the loneliness for those delights associated with the person. Divorced women have mentioned that they do not only miss their former husbands but also the lifestyle associated with them—theater, dinner, travel, meeting exciting people, doing exciting things. Most of these things came to an end with the divorce.

I tried to remember the last time I had seen Doug smile and wave to me as he went to the darkroom. If only I could go back and snap a picture of the last time and hang it on my wall. Perhaps that would help. On the other hand, it might make me feel even more lonely.

Each time we sat down to eat we stared at a vacant chair at the table. There were other vacant chairs, but they were supposed to be vacant. Sometimes it seemed that he should come through the front door while we were eating, apologize for being late, sit down in the vacant chair, and life would return to normal.

The emotional side of me almost expected it at times. But the rational side argued that it could never happen. I think the emotional side of me was hanging onto the comma at the end of his life, left dangling there because I never saw him dead. It's good that our rational side wins many of the arguments with our emotional side, isn't it? I would hate to think what would happen in my life if my emotional side won every argument.

I believe it was Aristotle who compared reason and emotion with two men driving a horse-drawn wagon. At times emotion grabs the reins and whips the horses into a frenzied gallop, taking wagon and drivers on a wild, crazy, dangerous ride. Then reason grabs the reins and things settle back to normal. In times of loneliness we need to pray earnestly for reason to hold the reins of our lives.

Weeks passed before Arlie and I could invade Doug's room and sort out his personal things. It was a task I dreaded, and I could seldom stay more than ten or fifteen minutes each time.

You learn much about your son when you enter the privacy of his room as he left it, expecting to be the next one to enter. I knew he was clean, orderly, and neat. But I had not realized before how orderly and well managed he was. I was embarrassed to find my son setting an example for me in something I should have exemplified for him.

There was nothing I was ashamed to find, nothing I would have been ashamed to leave behind if I were taken suddenly. One moment he left his room for a ball game. Weeks later we would enter that room exactly as he left it to sort out his things. It reminded me that each time I leave a room, leave friends, hug someone good-bye, leave my home, I should leave life in order. Someone else may be the next person to enter my inner sanctum to put my possessions in order or dispose of them.

Our family members have always respected one another's privacy. Doug's room was his private place, his refuge, his retreat, his own corner of the world where others, even his parents, came only by invitation. Respecting a child's room is an important dimension of respecting a child's personhood. Violate his privacy and you violate him. Now it seemed that we were violating his privacy, that we really shouldn't be in his room, handling his personal things, that we should be asking his permission even to step through the door.

Like the photos Arlie gathered, these personal effects were the only reflected images of the person. Handling the images without the person induced loneliness. They were a poor substitute for Doug.

But what we experienced is not unique to the death of a loved one. This could have been you or me in the room of a runaway, a child sent to prison, a husband or wife who ran off to marry another person, anyone who has left us with ourselves and our loneliness. Our search since then has been to turn our hurt of loneliness to healing. Perhaps that is your personal search also.

What is this mysterious nothingness we call loneliness? How do we lay hold of emptiness, a void, a concept without adequate definition? It's easy to say we are lonely because we miss someone. Of course we do. We miss that person's presence. We miss that person's warmth and words and ways. But loneliness is much more than missing someone. It is more than missing that person. It is also missing the sights, sounds, touch, and scents associated with that person. It is missing the familiar word spoken, the familiar ways, the familiar places associated with that person.

When I was a small boy, our family sat on the front porch of our farmhouse each evening after dinner. We talked together until bedtime. It is a forgotten chapter of Americana. Few families today have the time, schedule, or patience to do this each night. But these were postdepression years in rural America and farm families had no money to go anywhere. So we stayed home and talked. Looking back, I see our near-poverty as a blessing. Our conversations were ordinary. Some might think them too ordinary. But they communicated love among family members, a sense of belonging, a sense of withness.

Often the still evening air would be interrupted by the distant moan of a steam locomotive whistle, drifting across the rich prairie land. The railway cut across central Illinois in an east-west direction connecting villages and cities, hauling passengers and freight. When the wind came from the direction of the railway, we could hear the moaning whistle as the train made its way from my mother's childhood village of Fairmount to points east and west.

Often when the moaning sound drifted our way my mother would whisper, half to herself, half to anyone who listened, "It's so mournful." Then one evening I knew why. I remembered our visit to the family burial grounds in Fairmount, adjacent to these same railway tracks. My mother had buried her father and mother, her grandfather and grandmother, her brother and two babies in this cemetery by the railway tracks. Of course, the moaning whistle was not associated with the steam locomotive as much as the cemetery. It was a sound associated with family burials and the tears she had shed there. It was a lonely sound, not because the sound itself was lonely, but because she associated the sound with her loved ones.

I have often thought it strange how much people miss loved ones after they are gone, but did not seem to appreciate them when they were here. I was sure that one man I knew did not really care much about his wife, but when she died suddenly, he changed from a strong, invulnerable figure to a soft-hearted fellow who cried easily, especially when he thought about her.

Does loneliness bring into clear focus the love we did not know we had? Does it highlight qualities we did not appreciate? Does it bring into view a loved one's personal features we passed by in daily living? Must we lose someone to come to a full appreciation for that person, to know that we really did care for that person after all, to see clearly the true virtues we lived with each day but did not recognize?

We must not confuse loneliness with aloneness, or solitude. There is a time to be alone with God, a time to lay self before our Maker and in moments of solitude to seek his perspective on ourselves and our purposes. Solitude may have a restorative effect upon us while loneliness may have a draining effect. Solitude invites God's light to shine upon our souls to illuminate the dark corners. Loneliness sets our feet in those dark corners, then leaves us to brood. It is easy to be lonely when someone dies, truly lonely.

TURN YOUR LONELINESS INTO "WITHNESS"

Discovering New Meaning in Belonging

Toward the end of the last century, John George Rudy, a young Iowa pastor, became too sick to continue his work. In his desperate search for a better climate he traveled to California, hoping to get well and then return to his church, his wife, and his children, or bring them with him to a new life.

But John died and was buried northeast of San Francisco. It was not practical in those days for a penniless, pregnant widow like Katherine, with three children, to travel across the country to attend a funeral. Katherine was too poor to support her three children, with a fourth on the way. So her brother took her and her children in and they lived with him and his family.

In her lonely nothingness, Katherine made it the mission of her life to pray for her four small children and her unborn grandchildren. I knew each of her children as adults, for you see, one was my mother-in-law. All four were bathed in the presence of the Lord, bearing an aura of saintliness.

Katherine's seventeen grandchildren all married Christians and established Christian homes. Almost half of them entered some form of ministry. Of her fifty-seven great-grandchildren, those that I know of married Christians and established Christian homes. Quite a few are in some form of ministry.

Katherine had every right to feel lonely and isolated. It would have been tempting to crawl into a corner and complain about her bitter situation. Instead she reached out in the best way she could. In her situation, prayer was the only viable way of reaching out, so that was the way she did it. I know of people with chronic sickness who have carried out phone ministries. Others enjoy visiting those who need them.

Tragedy and loneliness need not be the end of the road. Instead, lonely people may find far-reaching ministry by reaching out to people who appreciate a loving word or a strong arm from someone else who has hurt.

Lifechanger 11
Coping with loneliness is not finding a substitute for the person you lost but finding new meaning for the person you are and the person you should be.

I have heard people speak of the hole left in their lives by the loss of a loved one. In one sense this is true, for that person occupied a time and place that no other person can fully occupy. It's like looking at the vacant chair across the table.

The person who sat there each mealtime is no longer there. The person who slept beside you, or in the next room, is no longer there. The person who talked with you, joked with you, worked with you, and traveled with you is gone. In one sense this loved one left a hole in your life.

But the problem with this idea is that we have a compulsion to fill holes with the same substance that we think was once there. There is something in us that cannot stand to leave a hole unfilled. A neighbor's dog gets into your yard and digs for a chipmunk. Your instinct tells you to fill the hole in the ground with dirt. Winter ice and snows make a hole in the pavement. You want your highway department to fill it with asphalt. Wherever we see holes, we feel we ought to fill them with what we think was once there. It's the proper thing to do. It rounds out life, makes it seem more complete.

Filling holes is easier in the lawn than in our lives. A couple I knew lost their baby in a tragic accident. Immediately they wanted another baby to fill up the hole left by the death of their child. They gave the second child a name that rhymed with the name of the first child. But of course the second child never really filled the hole left by the first. Parents can't forget one child by having another. Loved ones can't give up the sense of loss by gaining another family member.

Doug was a unique young man, with a distinct personality, a distinct relationship with each of us, a distinct mind, a distinct heart. If his death left a hole in us, it was a Doug-shaped hole. Trying to fill it is like trying to squeeze the proverbial square peg into a round hole. There is no other Doug-shaped person to fit exactly into a Doug-shaped hole.

Our thoughts about loneliness often center on this idea of a hole to be filled. If we can marry another person quickly after our mate dies or after we are divorced, if we can fill up our schedule with ceaseless activity, if we can buy a new house or take a long cruise, or do something to fill up our lives, it will take away our loneliness. We get the idea that loneliness is our response to a deserted inner landscape, deserted because someone we loved vacated the territory. If we can find someone or something to occupy the territory, we won't be lonely anymore. But it doesn't work that way.

When we made that loved one—child, husband, wife, business partner, friend—a significant other, we made that person part of our personal undivided wholeness. The territory Doug occupied was an undivided part of all of me, not merely one little compartment or room. If I had confined my son to one small compartment of my life I would have been a selfish father. I would not have known the true meaning of the father-son relationship. When I lost him, it would have damaged only that one compartment of my life, instead of a dimension of all my life.

But it wasn't that way. The territory he occupied was not one little tent out there somewhere, but the whole emotional plain. The loneliness brought about by his absence is not confined to one small part, but it stretches out over the undivided wholeness of my entire person. So I am dealing with the restoration of personal wholeness, not filling a hole, even a Doug-shaped hole.

Lifechanger 12
Coping with loneliness is not merely dealing with the pain of losing a loved one's presence but also confronting their absence as a new hostile presence.

In part, loneliness is the pain of absence, pain because we no longer have the warm, friendly presence of someone we

love. Even more, it is feeling the pain of a new presence. Death
is a presence. Loneliness is a presence. These unwanted, often
hostile, guests move into our personhood, pitch their tents,
and refuse to leave. We must deal with unseen, but powerful,
presences that want the undivided wholeness of our personhood. If we let them do it, they will. If there is a low place in
our lives, they will fill it.

Lifechanger 13
*Turn your lonely memories of the past into
productive visions for the future.*

But trying to fill our lives with people, activity, or things
cannot compete with these fearsome presences. If surrounding ourselves with people is the answer to loneliness,
we should never be lonely in a crowd. The loneliest place on
earth is not a desert where there are no people but a room or
street crowded with strangers who care little if you live or die.
Loneliness may be initiated by the absence of those who care,
but it is not resolved by the presence of those who don't care.

You and I face the task of recognizing what we lost, not
merely someone who was important to us, but someone who
was part of us. I lost a son, but I lost much more—an undivided part of all of me—and that can't be filled with another
person, another activity, another house, another location, or
another job. I can't restore Doug to me but I must restore
myself to me. I cannot cope with the new presences that
moved into my life; I must invite an even greater Presence in
to deal with them, the person of Jesus Christ.

Arlie began a book of memories, with hundreds of photos
I had taken since Doug's birth, mementos he and we had gathered that would help to reconstruct his life. These were but

images of a once-vibrant life and each brought a stream of memories flowing into a river of loneliness.

I learned that the therapy of remembering past blessings brings with it the pain of realizing that past blessings are indeed past. If we leave things there, dwelling only on the past, we can drift into depression and something dies within us. It would have been easy to sit there all day, perhaps every day, and cry because there would be no more pictures added to the albums. Doug would not have been pleased to see us do that, and I would not be pleased if I thought my survivors would do that someday.

If you have lost someone—through death, divorce, broken communications, or whatever the reason—and you are dwelling only in the past, you are watering, fertilizing, and cultivating a decaying seed. No fresh green plant for future harvest will grow from that. If you are to turn your hurts into healing, you must do all you can to help the seeds of past blessings germinate and grow toward a harvest of future blessings.

Of course we must grieve. Of course we return to the past to remember good things. But there comes a time to nurture the seeds of yesterday to assure a generous harvest tomorrow.

We appreciate our book of memories, not because it helps us dwell on the past, not because it gives us something to cry about, not because it is a salve for loneliness, but because it helps us in the continuing celebration of life. Each memento reminds us again that life in its fullness, with God, is something to celebrate. Even small failures and things we wish we had done, things that nag and irritate, can be celebrated, for they can become important nutrients in producing a future harvest.

I had forgotten so many things we did together, so many small details fade in the passage of time. I had forgotten exactly what he looked like each year, almost each month of each year. I had forgotten the things I wished we had done together, the things we had planned to do but time or circumstance had kept us from doing.

I could dwell on things we didn't do and forget the things we did do. I could cry about things left undone and fail to remember father-son accomplishments. That would be cultivating a rotting seed. Instead, I must spend my energies encouraging younger parents to spend time with their children, do things with them, have fun with them; then the seeds planted in our memory book can grow to a harvest in children I don't even know.

Each photo makes our hearts ache because he isn't here, but each brings us renewed joy because he *was* here for twenty-six years. I will celebrate the twenty-six years he was with us rather than lament the next twenty-six years he will not be with us. I will celebrate who he was and what he did rather than lament what he could have become and what he could have achieved.

We have determined that we will not sit by the pit of loneliness and cry our lives away. Instead, we will pray and work so that the seeds of our son's death will germinate, bring forth vibrant shoots of hope, and produce a good harvest in other lives, perhaps even those we will never meet.

Lifechanger 14
The best antidote to loneliness is the Lord's "withness."

Two of the loneliest words in the English language are *abandon* and *forsake*. There is a plaintive quality to those words for they suggest someone you love leaving you alone.

Did my son Doug forsake me? No, not at all. He did not choose to leave Arlie and me alone. He was taken. He did not go away by choice.

But what about a young man I'll call Charles? He told his young pregnant wife that he doesn't want her or his child. He wants to have his freedom. Charles is forsaking his wife and his child. He is abandoning them. There are hundreds of thousands of men and women out there like Charles. You know some of them. They want out. They don't want the responsibility of marriage. They want to play. For the pleasure of playing, they are willing to abandon, forsake, someone who loves them.

Charles and his counterparts are selfish people. They are abandoning a loved one not in the interests of that loved one but in the purely selfish interests of pleasure, the pleasure of playing around. The word *commitment* is a foreign word to Charles and his friends. Commitment says, "I will be with you in sickness and in health, in wealth or poverty, when the feelings are there or when they have waned, in sunshine or shadow, in joy or sorrow."

Wedding vows are vows of commitment, withness no matter what, withness even when I don't feel like it. The winds of changing feelings that blow across the surface of our lives will not cause me to forsake you.

The loneliness we faced when we lost our son was withoutness. We were lonely because he wasn't there anymore. We were lonely because the delightful things associated with him were not there anymore.

But the loneliness of some of our divorced friends is much more than withoutness. They have that too. But divorced people who have been forsaken, abandoned, have a more intense loneliness than ours. They have been told, by word or by conduct, "You are no longer of value to me. I don't need you or want you anymore."

It's easy to cross over from "no longer of value to me" to "no longer of value." Self-esteem is on the line. Self-worth is damaged. It is no longer a matter of withoutness, being without a loved one who mattered, but the rejected person has been devalued in the process. So that leaves the rejected person without a loved one and without a proper value on his or her own personhood. It's a double loss.

Parents of runaways face the double loss also—they have lost a child (at least for the time), and they have lost credibility as a parent. "What did we do wrong?" is an easy question to ask. Actually the parent may not have done anything wrong. Children do get in with the wrong crowd. But sometimes the parent recognizes that he or she has not always shared his or her withness with the child, so now the child is withdrawing withness.

The Lord summarizes his withness in a name—*Immanuel,* which means, "God with us" (see Isa. 7:14; 8:8; Matt. 1:23). Immanuel is the model for husbands, wives, mothers, fathers, and all others who pledge withness. God with us is more than an observer, a spectator in the heavenly grandstand, observing our struggles on the playing field of life. His withness is on the team; he is down on the field with us, a player coach of sorts, involved with us on a game-by-game, play-by-play basis. He is there with us and our win is his win, our loss is his loss. He said, through Moses, "The Lord himself goes before you and will be with you; he will never leave you nor forsake you. Do not be afraid; do not be discouraged" (Deut. 31:8).

The Lord goes beyond the name of withness, *Immanuel.* The gospel is the Good News of the Lord personalizing withness. It is hard to understand God with us since we can't see

him, can't touch him. God sent Immanuel in the flesh, his Son
Jesus, so that now we could see God with us, and as John
wrote, "That which was from the beginning, which we have
heard, which we have seen with our eyes, which we have
looked at and our hands have touched—this we proclaim concerning the Word of life" (1 John 1:1).

But the Lord's withness does not stop with the name, or
with his presence in flesh, but continues on throughout our
pilgrimage here on earth, as he promised in the Great Commission, "Go and make disciples of all nations. . . . And surely
I will be with you always, to the very end of the age" (Matt.
28:19–20).

The Lord's withness is the very opposite of abandonment
or forsakenness. When we are abandoned by someone we
love, we are cut off from that love, depreciated in value, isolated from that personhood. The Lord's withness bonds us to
his love, enhances our personal value, and makes us one with
his Personhood. Jesus said, "Because I live, you also will live.
. . . You will realize that I am in my Father, and you are in me,
and I am in you" (John 14:19–20).

The Gospel story pulls aside the curtain of mystery and
reveals God suffering for us on the cross. It reveals his suffering within two parentheses of time, from Jesus' birth in
Bethlehem until his ascension on the Mount of Olives. But it
indirectly reveals the Lord suffering for his people beyond
these two parentheses. God is love, and suffering and love
are inseparable.

SUFFERING

Digging for Thorns
As They Go Deeper

The abrupt loss of a significant person interrupts the flow of life like a commanding statement set between two parentheses. After the final parenthesis life resumes its restless flow, but the flow is changed, altered significantly by what was said, what transpired, within the parentheses. Life goes on, but it isn't the same because you and I were changed significantly between the parentheses.

During my week between two parentheses I had totally forgotten what was in my datebook. I had even forgotten that I had a datebook. Furthermore, I didn't care if I had a datebook.

But on Sunday, the day after Doug's funeral, I remembered that domineering little book that prefers to be master rather than servant, and discovered that I was scheduled the next morning for a radio interview on Moody's WMBI, a program called "Speaking of Books." A week later I was to go to Lan-

caster for two days of author appearances at the Provident
Bookstores.

So soon? I really didn't want to do either. I didn't want to
jump back into the demands of life so quickly. Since Wednesday night, when Arlie and I had cried in each other's arms at
our cottage, we had been on a ceaseless carousel ride of hurts
and tears, but always with others. We had not had time to ponder and reflect on twenty-six years of memories with Doug.
We had been thrust between the parentheses with rude
abruptness and now we were being thrust out in the same way.

Should I call in the morning and cancel the interview? If I
did, why was I doing it? What would I tell the interviewers?
That I just didn't want to do it? That I deserved to stay home
because I had buried my son two days earlier? That I wanted
to stay home and cry?

If I canceled the interview, should I also cancel the Provident appearances? What about the family outing at Turkey
Run, Indiana, in less than three weeks? There was a steady
stream of things like that. I could cancel things indefinitely,
but at what point would I no longer have an excuse to cancel
responsibility?

An inner referee blew the whistle on me—God's people are
called to serve at all times, not only on sunny days. Suffering
is no excuse for not serving. Quite the opposite, suffering is
an opportunity for service, for fellow sufferers could now
relate to me. I remembered that our tears can be an offering
to God, but only if they are offered *for* something, *for* someone. God does not accept our tears as an offering if they keep
us *from* his business.

I knew Doug's thinking on these matters, much like my
own. I would be disgusted, perhaps a bit angry, if I thought
my loved ones had opportunities for Christian service the

week after my funeral and chose instead to sit in a corner and cry. I would not be at all happy to think that my death, my graduation into the presence of the Lord, had prevented them from serving that same Lord.

Yes, life committed to serve must resume because to serve is to live. My tears must not prevent me from serving but rather grace my serving, making me a more effective servant, a more understanding servant.

I also determined that I must not weep for Doug, for he was in the King's presence. I must not weep for myself, or encourage others to feel sorry for me. I must not even cry to stroke myself, for that is self-pity. But I thought it right to weep for my loss, a significant part of myself lost when I lost my son. I am weeping because I miss him as part of me, I am less than myself without him, the experiences I enjoyed with him are no longer there.

I weep because I must learn how to adjust myself to become a different whole person without a significant other who helped me to be that whole person. It is I who will never be the same with an important part of me gone, and in my tears I seek to adjust a new me into old familiar paths of serving. I will never be the same whole person that I was when Doug was alive, because my wholeness included him. But I can become a new and equally effective whole person, a different whole person. I must become whole again, with Doug's memory as part of me instead of Doug. We who survive owe it to Doug to make his death at least as redemptive as his life.

This is the suffering of surviving, the suffering of looking at new responsibilities with a new face. This is also the responsibility of surviving.

As a survivor I must also try to sort out why I am a survivor and what I should do about it. One person was taken and another not. I could easily think it unfair that I, a middle-aged man, was continuing business as usual, while Doug, a young man in his prime, had abruptly terminated all business here on earth. But what if I had died instead of Doug? He would likely think it unfair that a husband and breadwinner was taken while he, unmarried with no dependents, was left behind.

Trying to understand the essence of fairness is like trying to analyze pure justice. Sometimes it is more important in this world of unexplainable uncertainty to learn to adjust than to understand. In God's home later we will look back and understand. Now I must seek to understand what I can, and content myself to adjust to those matters beyond the boundaries of human understanding.

In the abrupt appearance of sudden tragedy we have little time to ponder these things. Later, floodgates open to release a thousand conflicts within. Wars break out within our souls as we struggle to cope with a survivor's suffering. We grieve or mourn and wonder why. It is trying to live with loss, the disruptive loss of a significant other person, who was also part of me.

I mourn, not because Doug has graduated into the palace of the King, but because he has left me, and in leaving me, he has left me less than the whole person I was. I mourn, not because Doug has gone to live with God, but because he has left me here to cope with my new incompleteness. I mourn, not for Doug, but for me. So it is I who must heal, and I must heal by learning to become a whole person again, a different whole person from the one I was before.

The weekend following my trip to Lancaster our family trooped valiantly to Turkey Run State Park for our annual traditional family weekend. The Turkey Run experience has become a non-negotiable, hidebound tradition, a commitment we maintain to one another. We make reservations as far ahead as they will accept them.

This tradition is a given; no one would think of stopping it because no one wants to stop it. We *will* be there together each October. Nothing will keep one of us away, except this year something will keep one of us away.

It almost seemed that God should give Doug a leave of absence from heaven for that weekend to be with us. But part of mourning is the recognition of the great gulf that loss excavates between us. The bridge across the gulf is one way only! For the first time since he was a little boy, Doug would not be with us. The pain of his absence would be.

Now, exactly three weeks after Doug's funeral, his empty place would shout at us. We were painfully aware that we would come face to face with his absence on every trail, at every meal, at every log or rock where we stopped to talk or pray or laugh. His absence would not be something missing as much as something present to aggravate our suffering, to pour salt in raw wounds.

Not one of us thought we should cancel Turkey Run any more than we should cancel other significant appointments. The Turkey Run experience had become a form of service through the years, the service of commitment, a daring statement to one another that "I will be with you, no matter what." If more families made that uncompromising commitment to one another, we could dispense with half our Christian organizations and their buildings and programs. We wouldn't need them. Their ministries would be ingrained already in the family woodwork.

During these days of hurt I tried to think what I would want the family to do if I had been the one taken in the car accident. I would want them to resume life, abundant life. I would want them to adjust to the new wholeness necessary to live without me. Of course they could mourn their loss, their own adjustment, but certainly not me. How could they mourn for me when I have gone into the presence of the Lord? Mourning must not be for the Christian who has joined the Lord. Mourning is the process of learning new wholeness.

If I were the one taken, I would want my survivors to resume life with zest and joy. I would want them to enter into the arena of life again to fulfill their mission on earth, to be the servants God wants them to be, and to fulfill their mourning for their loss so they can serve effectively. But withdraw from the mainstream of life? How could they pay tribute to me by withdrawing from the kind of joyful living I had worked so hard to instill in them? This is my public statement to them now.

I knew that's how Doug would think because we had talked about these kinds of things. The best tribute, the finest service in my memory, or Doug's memory, is to continue the commitments that welded our family together, but present them as an offering to God and a memorial to Doug. To withdraw from the Turkey Run custom, or any other wholesome, joyful experience would be to violate what each of us had committed ourselves to build in one another.

An outsider visiting our tradition for a weekend might think it too ordinary. We're not producing anything, not earning anything, not investing in anything, not building anything, not creating anything. But of course that isn't true because we are producing family unity, earning the right to be called family, investing in the future security of the family, building a family infrastructure that will help us withstand the storms of life, and creating a trust that says "I will be with you. That is my commitment to you. Nothing and no one will take me from you."

The Turkey Run tradition must be replayed, even though we all knew we would suffer from replaying it without a key character who made it the fixed tradition that it is. It was like trying to drive a car with the speedometer missing, or eating dinner with silverware missing. But we must drive the car or eat our dinner. We'll do it, but it takes some major adjustment in ourselves.

We must have time to mourn a tragic loss. Jesus said, "Blessed are those who mourn, for they will be comforted" (Matt. 5:4). No mourning, no blessing. He was not saying that we are blessed to have a loss so we can mourn but that we are blessed by mourning when we have a loss. The blessing is in renewing our walk with God as we strive to understand how he has interwoven the threads of love and loss and mourning and comfort for that mourning.

Arlie and I had been on the run since the night we learned of Doug's fatal accident. When we returned home from Turkey Run, we expected that we could begin to sift the ashes of our tragedy, search for something redemptive in our loss, to begin the necessary process of mourning.

But our expectation was short-lived. Another unbelievably painful tragedy was around the corner, another thorn was poised to strike into our hearts, a ton of bricks was about to fall upon us with no warning.

Shortly after Doug's accident we had received a letter from the coroner's office, advising us that there would be a routine hearing to determine the cause of the accident and that we would be advised so that we could participate. But no notice ever came.

Two days after we returned from Turkey Run, on Tuesday night, we opened the local newspaper. A rather lengthy article screamed at us—the coroner's jury had met without us! They had ruled Doug's death "accidental suicide." With no one there to explain the sudden seizures precipitated by the bump on the head Doug received from his previous accident, they didn't know what to do with the evidence. The raw facts, a car smashing into a brick wall, appeared to be suicide. But the small amount of character reference that was presented by the detective suggested a person who would not commit suicide. So they issued a verdict that said both. But the word *suicide* shouts infinitely louder than *accidental*.

The pain of loss was enough. Now the pain of having Doug's character stained with the word *suicide* poured the salt of agony in the raw wounds of loss. We can handle honorable loss of life better than we can handle the dishonorable loss of reputation. Furthermore, one harsh word like *suicide* prevails over a hundred kind words like *accidental*. Say a hundred loving words to your mate today, but you will cancel them all out with one harsh word. Live a lifetime of gracious, steady, productive, exemplary conduct and the press will ignore you. But one fling in a thoughtless moment, one night on the town, and no one remembers the lifetime of exemplary conduct. The word *suicide* would give us a lifetime of hurt unless we could erase it.

Almost as painful was the abrasive way the young reporter presented the account. Doug had been quite visible in local and state politics—campaign manager for two state senators, precinct captain, candidate for the state legislature. This reporter was not content to report the ruling but embellished the article with a long list of innuendo, half-truth, and blatant error. He painted Doug grossly out of character. Instead of a strong Christian leader that we and Doug's acquaintances knew him to be, he was portrayed as a foolish kid who had committed suicide because he lost a softball game. On that dark day, the reporter had access to the eyes, and indirectly the judgment, of the public through the newspaper, and I did not.

I had never before realized that agony of loss can so quickly be transcended by the agony of misunderstanding, misrepresentation, and rejection. Now I understood a little better the agony of the cross, Jesus' greater agony, not merely dying, but dying as an act of love for those who were killing him as an act of hatred. Jesus went to the cross to die for people, all of us, who would send him to the cross. How can love reach out to embrace the arm that is poised to maim or kill the very one offering love? Only the love of Christ, the love shown on the cross, can do that. But that same love is lived out through his followers, even two millennia after that transcending act of redemptive splendor.

The agony of that dark Tuesday night swept over us like some enormous tidal wave, unsuspected, unannounced, and unmerciful. Who should we call, and what should we do to begin to correct this horrible report? I have wondered since how many innocent people have lost their reputations, and with them their self-esteem, through irresponsible reporting. What would a young reporter gain from embellishing an already painfully inaccurate verdict? I suppose a moment of glee, or whatever small reward there was in making another young man look ridiculous. But what would a family face if they could not correct that report? A lifetime of hurt and agony. It was like burning a cathedral to fry an egg, a dear price to pay for a moment of questionable gratification. It was an expensive reminder to me to seek the mind of Christ when dealing with the reputations of my fellow pilgrims.

I think neither of us slept through that long dark night. We wanted to call someone—the newspaper editor, the coroner's office, the reporter, members of the jury, the detective. We wanted to shout for all the world to hear, "You don't know this young man that we knew so well. He wouldn't even *think* of taking his own life! He had no reason to do that, and if he did have a reason, suicide would not have been an option for him."

The one moment of hope that evening was dinner with our friends Will and Ginny Hohm. Will, a medical doctor, explained to us how the bump Doug received from his previous accident had likely caused the seizures that he began having the next week. He explained how something had probably precipitated a seizure the night Doug was driving home, and his body became rigid, forcing his foot against the accelerator. Doug became a passenger in his own car, barely able to steer it but unable to relax his rigid leg and remove his foot from the accelerator. Dr. Hohm said he would be glad to explain all of this to the coroner's jury if we could get it to convene again. But a coroner's jury is not easily reconvened. We knew that.

An attorney friend, Howard Broecker, pursued the matter and won a new inquest for December 11. We faced almost two months of agonizing uncertainty. We were determined with all our hearts, minds, and strength to clear Doug's good name and reputation, and we would devote ourselves with all our energies to that purpose.

We prepared for this simple inquest with vigor, as though our lives depended on it. In a very real sense, they did, for if we lost this struggle, a lifetime of grief for a lost son would be compounded by a lifetime of aggravated grief for his stained reputation. During those weeks we had to suspend mourning, put it on hold, set it on the back burner while we invested all our thoughts and energies into the task at hand, clearing the record and Doug's reputation with it.

The courtroom was filled the day of the inquest, mostly with character witnesses—a state senator, a regional transportation authority board member, a political science professor, attorney friends, a doctor, and one of Doug's high school teachers. Through his visible involvement in political campaigns, Doug had won the respect and love of many community and state leaders. Each witness spoke of impeccable character, a young man of purpose and integrity. How different from the foolish young man portrayed by the press, a spoiled kid who would drive his car into a brick wall because he lost a softball game! I recognized this young man I heard about at the inquest. The person created by the press was a total stranger.

Arlie and I were tense throughout the inquest. We had lost our son. We *couldn't* see his character maligned publicly! Dr. Will Hohm clearly presented insights about seizures, how they can be precipitated and how they can cause an accident like Doug's. Howard Broecker did his work with gracious firmness. The witnesses who knew Doug well portrayed him as we knew him. Perhaps thirty or forty people were there that day to testify concerning Doug's stature and good character.

At last the moment for the verdict came. We had postponed mourning for two months to prepare for this moment. Would the jury see what the rest of us saw so clearly?

The foreman rose and read the verdict—"accidental." We breathed a sigh of relief. Now I wanted to release the emotion that had been welled up in me for almost two months. The tears had been dammed up all this time, trying to burst out, but the preoccupation with clearing Doug's name had left no time or energy to shed them.

Some jury members came to me after the inquest and graciously apologized for the needless pain that had been thrust upon us. It had not been their fault. They had worked with what they had, and with no one to come to Doug's defense two months earlier, they gave the ambivalent decision that plagued us when we should have been mourning instead.

During the years when my children were growing up, I dug many thorns from their hands. Perhaps you have done this too. Sometimes a thorn was buried deep in the flesh. The more I dug for it, the deeper it seemed to go. Pain and suffering were compounded for the poor child.

The pain I inflicted by digging for the thorn added to the pain the thorn brought in the first place. It is the salt-in-raw-wound syndrome. Pain exacerbated by further pain, often needless. That is the portrait of Doug's death and the suffering it brought to us—pain inflicted not only by his death but compounded by our not being there when it happened, accented by our not seeing him dead, aggravated by burying him in the rain, rubbed raw by the accusation of suicide, magnified by an abrasive news report, intensified by two months of preparing for a new inquest, brought to a burning focus by the inquest itself.

Wasn't it enough to lose a son? But through this salt-in-raw-wound syndrome, this layer upon layer of pain, we learned also that pain can have its purpose. It can be *for* something.

TURN YOUR PAIN
INTO PURPOSE

Exploring the Other Side of Suffering

This world was fashioned by the all-wise Creator. I assume he knew what he was doing. I hope you assume that too. If God had delegated creation to me, I would have tried to create a utopia, a little heaven on earth. There would be no place for thorns or weeds. I would have outlawed disease and injury. Germs and viruses would have to go. There would be no insects, no flies, no mosquitoes, probably no bees if I had been stung recently. I would have mandated fairness and justice, love and mercy, obedience and honesty, and all other good qualities. Everyone would have to exercise virtue because vice would not be permitted.

I think God knew more about creation than I. So he created thorns and weeds and germs and viruses. He made mosquitoes and flies and snakes and toads. He made tonsils and an appendix for each person. We don't know why he made some of these things, but he did, so we assume there was a purpose.

God also created a quality in human behavior called choice—the option to sin and be unjust and mean-spirited. He didn't tell us to be that way, but he left room for us to be ourselves instead of zombies or clones made from one rigid pattern.

So in his wonderful creation, God left room for us to enter into life's adventure with a zest, and that also gives us the option to be hurt. With that gift of choice, we may choose to sin, which also is a choice to be hurt and to hurt others, even to hurt God. With that choice we may also choose to be what he knows we should be, which may also help others be what he knows they should be.

God left a margin in human behavior to be decent, and loving, and law abiding, and kind to one another. He didn't mandate love and decency and kindness, but he left room for us to live beyond ourselves. He created a remarkable option to be transhuman, to rise above the human norm, and to be godly, not only to pattern our conduct after God, but to draw from God's resources to make this conduct God-like.

God never gives us the option to be God, or even to possess certain unique attributes that only God can have—such as perfection, full control over our destiny without outside help, or unlimited power. But he does help us to become God-like, or godly, and that quality of conduct and thinking is transhuman, above normal human conduct. I would not have thought of that option in creation. I would have made people to be the very best people they could be—no options to be more or less. But God arranged for us to become much less than that or much more than that. Godliness is beyond human thinking. It is a new paradigm of thought. To think godliness, you must think about God. To cultivate godliness, you must walk daily with God. You cannot conceive of godliness while you depend on human behavior alone.

In my creative thoughtfulness, I would have narrowed the options for life. Life at its best would be one grand vacation, with the sun always shining and things always going our way. Pain and suffering would not have been an option. It would not have been a part of my small-minded creation.

I think you should be glad that God did not delegate the act of creation to me—or to you. On rainy days, when we're sick in bed, or we have lost our jobs or have become the victims of injustice, we may be tempted to think we could improve on creation. Swarms of mosquitoes or flies invading our patio can also tempt us to think that way. If you and I are tempted to think we can improve on God's creative genius, we underestimate God or overestimate ourselves.

The following lifechangers have changed my own view of suffering as part of God's creation. Perhaps they will change your life too.

Lifechanger 15
Love and suffering are two sides of the same coin. You cannot love without getting hurt and you should not get hurt without discovering new dimensions of love.

Doug's death introduced a new perspective of suffering into my life. The trauma of the accident, the layers of pain in subsequent events, the wounds that remain—all speak eloquently of suffering, a type of suffering I had never before encountered. I have asked myself why all of this hurt so much and the answer is that I loved so much. To the degree that I loved my son, I suffered because of his loss. If I had kept my son at a distance, had not learned to love him, his loss would not have brought so much pain. Love, loss, and pain are all weighed on the same scales.

If you are a husband or wife, you know that love in the marriage relationship can bring suffering. When you love someone, and live with that person daily, you will get hurt. The little things we say and do, and often the little things we neglect to say and do, bring pain to one another.

Divorce, the ultimate brokenness of the marriage relationship, brings unbelievable pain. The pain it brings is intimately related to the bond of love that once held the marriage together. When the bond of love that holds a marriage together is not the love between husband and wife but the love of one mate for the lifestyle provided by the other, or the love of one mate for the children, or the love of one mate for God, or for something else, it is easier for that marriage to come unglued. True love, the love known as commitment, is the valid glue that binds marriage partners together.

A completely loveless marriage (one that lacks love, not only for a mate but for anything else associated with the marriage) should be relatively painless to dissolve. Let's assume, for example, a marriage without children, with no love between mates, and with no lifestyle consideration, and neither person cares what God thinks about all this. If this marriage dissolves, is there much hurt? Probably not, because there was no love. Why should there be pain if there was never love to give birth to pain? Love is the birthing grounds for pain. Love is the womb in which pain is conceived and grows.

The principal reason you hurt when you lose a marriage partner is because you loved your mate. Of course you enjoyed other things associated with the marriage. To the degree that love is lacking between mates, pain of dissolution is lacking too. Perhaps that is one reason divorce comes easily to many marriages today—there was little true love (commitment) to begin with.

People who get divorced from a mate they never loved but feel pain because they lost something else important to them (child, convictions, lifestyle) may try to ease their pain by seeking to replace what they did not want to lose, rather than the mate they wanted to lose.

We must be sure to distinguish true love from mere feelings. Mates who divorce when feelings wane may feel pain because they gave up someone they truly love. They think they no longer love someone, but they do. Feelings are like the waves upon the ocean, affected by every changing wind. Love is like the tides that do not change with fickle winds.

Ruptured love of a parent for a child, or a child for a parent, can generate intense pain. When a parent breaks a child's trust, the child experiences pain. Perhaps the parent drinks too much, spends too much time in a career and too little time with the child, or never shows a personal interest in the child. This is painful for the child because a child naturally wants to love the parent, and wants the parent to love him too.

On the other hand, the child may break the parent's heart and inflict pain. Running away is a common source of pain inflicted on parents. The child who refuses to obey parents, or constantly argues with parents, or makes fun of parents is a source of pain because the parent loves the child and wants the child to love him too.

Imagine the parental type of pain you and I have brought to the heart of God! God has suffered much at our hands, and we will not understand that unless one of our children has done that to us.

Since I was a boy, I have often quoted the all-time favorite verse, John 3:16. Perhaps you have quoted it many times also. We learn to say it quickly, pass over the meaning without thinking it through. As I have thought about the pain I must have brought to the heart of God, I reconsidered John 3:16. "For God so loved the world [substitute your name for *world*], that he gave his only begotten son [do you love anyone enough to give your son for that person?], that whosoever believeth ... should not perish, but have everlasting life [a gift of splendor for ordinary people]" (KJV).

Everlasting life, a life that never ends, is a splendid gift, a gift of splendor, not merely because this gift of never-ending life is very valuable, but because God gave you this gift personally, hand to hand, heart to heart. Even more, it is a gift of splendor, not merely because God gave it to you personally, but because it cost God something very precious to give it to you. The splendor of his gift came from the splendor of his sacrificial love.

The love with which God gave his wonderful gift was splendid, not because it was free of pain and suffering, but because God suffered pain, paid a great personal price of suffering, in order to give it. "Christ suffered for you, leaving you an example, that you should follow in his steps" (1 Peter 2:21).

Christ's steps that we are to follow are those of loving suffering, paying the price to give our loving gift.

If we would understand the depths of pain and suffering, we must first look into the face of love. Looking into the face of bitterness and hatred makes suffering even more unreasonable. It is a dead-end street with a dark pit at the end.

John 3:16 wouldn't make sense if it said, "For God so loved the world, but he would not give . . ."

Lifechanger 16
Majesty and loving suffering are two
threads in the same tapestry. Suffering by
itself is lonely and bitter, but suffering inter-
woven with love is a sacrificial gift.

Through my growing-up years I resisted the imagery of blood sacrifices in the Old Testament. Yes, of course, I believed that God had established them. But as a boy growing up on a farm, killing animals was a blood-splattering, unpleasant act. Since we depended on our farm animals for food, I witnessed many animal killings and I found it hard to associate these with worship. It seemed better to me to worship God in other ways, in the quietness of our village church, for example.

During my boyhood years, we did not go to the butcher shop or supermarket for meat. Chickens were a favorite food, especially in warmer months when it was not practical, without refrigeration, to butcher a large animal, such as a calf or hog.

The worst part for me was watching the animal killed. My mother was quite good at wringing a chicken's neck. To her that was the humane way to do it. Whenever she passed a butcher shop in town, she complained about the "inhumane" way the butcher killed the chickens, by sticking a knife in the brain. It seemed to me that there was no humane way to kill a chicken, but I certainly enjoyed eating the meat.

I think it was the blood that bothered me. If you have ever watched a chicken whose neck has been wrung, you know what I mean. The headless carcass does a remarkable dance for a minute or two, with blood splattering from the neck on anything nearby. It's not the kind of scene you would invite your friends or neighbors to watch. You would not tell them, "Dress up in your best and come to our chicken killing." You wouldn't!

But you would invite your friends or neighbors to dress up and come to your chicken dinner. There is something majestic about a beautiful platter of chicken or turkey gracing the center of the dinner table. The majestic focal point of Thanksgiving dinner is that beautiful turkey that required so much work to prepare. Think how unmajestic Thanksgiving dinner would be if you seated your guests at the table, lit the candles, played soft music, then brought out paper plates with a couple of raw carrots on each one.

The majesty is in the bird, not in its slaughtering but in its gracing the dinner table. Or is that true? Is not the majesty also in the sacrifice, the gift of life for us, both in the yard and on the table?

It's not easy for me to think of that bloody, dancing carcass as part of majesty. But at that moment life was being expended so that other life could continue. The chicken was relinquishing life so that my life might be sustained. The slaughtering was not of itself majestic, but the relinquishing of life was, especially relinquishing life to sustain life.

Was that perhaps the majesty of the blood sacrifices of the Old Testament? In the absence of, and anticipation of, Christ's once-for-all relinquishing of life for life, God established a prototype of life for life. It wasn't much, of course, the gift of a mere sheep for the sins of people. But it was as good as the gift of a chicken's life to sustain mine. And it did speak of that infinitely more majestic gift to come, the life of God's Son for the eternal life of mere people.

The majesty of Christ's loving offering of himself was not merely that one life was given for another life, but that the life of God's Son was given for mere humans. Not only that, but the life of God's Son was given for sinful humans, the just for the unjust. Instead of the sheep dying for the people, the lesser for the greater, as in the Old Testament sacrificial system, here we have the greater (God's Son) dying for the lesser (his people), and not only the lesser, but the undeserving lesser (sinners).

Lifechanger 17

Love is a sacrifice of suffering. Sacrificial suffering and love are two companions on the same road. You cannot truly walk with one without walking with the other.

Suppose God said to you, "I love you, I really do. But don't ask me to do anything big for you. Don't ask me to give my Son for you!" We would have to take John 3:16 out of the Bible, wouldn't we? We would have to remove communion. In fact, we would delete the entire gospel. There would be no Good News. The Good News is that God loved you so much that he made a sacrificial offering of his Son. He suffered sacrificially for you.

I have heard men quote Ephesians 5:22 as though it stands alone in that chapter. "Wives, submit to your husbands as to the Lord." Submission is love, a form of sacrificial love. It's there. God asks, no commands, wives to do it "as to the Lord." It's an act of submission to the Lord as well as to the husband. But it's also an act of submission as if she were submitting to the Lord. Submission to abuse and destructive behavior is not submitting "as to the Lord." He's not that way.

Also, Ephesians 5:22 walks hand in hand with Ephesians 5:25–27, "Husbands, love your wives, just as Christ loved the church and gave himself up for her to make her holy, cleansing her by the washing with water through the word, and to present her to himself as a radiant church, without stain or wrinkle or any other blemish, but holy and blameless." The husband's commitment is to (1) love his wife, (2) love his wife as Christ loved the church, (3) love his wife enough to die for her, (4) give himself to the task of helping his wife become a radiant, holy, blameless person. The wife is to submit herself to her husband in this task.

Is the wife's role of submission to the husband's task a sacrificial role? Yes, it takes submission and sacrificial love to submit, even to a noble purpose like that. Is the husband's role of love sacrificial? Yes, his task outlined above requires much sacrificial love.

Husband and wife will suffer much in fulfilling what is actually a mutual task—building one another in the Lord, cleansing one another for the Lord, sacrificially loving one another as to the Lord.

The marriage that works is the one in which each mate sacrifices self for the other. Sacrifice is costly, hurtful, painful. But it is pain and hurt and cost offered up like a burnt offering of old for the other person.

Parents and children have a similar relationship. The parent-child relationship that succeeds is the one in which both parent and child sacrifices self for each other. That too is costly, hurtful, painful. But it also is offered up like a burnt offering to the other person.

Think of an exemplary family that you know. You will find sacrificial love for others in the family. Think of a family you know that is pulling apart. Is the sacrificial love missing, the love that suffers hurt and pain to build others in the family?

Christian history is filled with examples of sacrificial suffering to express love, because Christ throughout the last two thousand years has touched people with the spirit of his own sacrificial suffering to express love. Dozens of Christian churches, schools, missions, and parachurch organizations have been founded, not to make the founders comfortable but to give them an opportunity to suffer in love for Christ.

Two names come to mind, Mother Teresa, who buried her life in the streets of Calcutta to minister to suffering people, and Charles Colson, who suffered much during his own imprisonment, but when he was released, returned again and again to minister to prisoners. Each person has suffered much, sacrificially giving self away. That kind of sacrifice is called love.

Does God send tragedy to help us become more effective servants? Possibly. But the real issue is not whether God sends tragedy but what we do with tragedy when it comes. I believe that the loss of someone we love, or even something we love, is a challenge to serve God and others more effectively because we now are sensitized to the sacrifice of suffering.

Lifechanger 18
Suffering and creation are interwoven. Creation without suffering would be sterile and valueless. Matters of significance are significant because they cost something.

I have never been pregnant, but Arlie has—five times. It is an uncomfortable experience I am told, filled with risk. Fewer women die in childbirth today than in earlier times, but some still do. Becoming pregnant is putting life on the line. It is suffering discomfort, living with awkwardness, watching diet, and changing daily habits during the nine months while the fetus is in the womb.

Each time a child was born, I waited anxiously to visit Arlie in the hospital room. When she held our newborn baby in her arms, she always wore a radiant smile, a smile of triumph and satisfaction. There was a glow that said, "I'm worn out from it all, but so satisfied." She walked through the valley of self-sacrifice, pain, and suffering, even through the valley of the shadow of death, and had come out the other side victorious.

Of course that was only the beginning of a lifetime of service to that child. There would be nursing, changing diapers, bathing, teaching the child to walk, toilet training, music lessons, school lunches to make, counseling, correcting, encouraging, chauffeuring, attending recitals and Little League games, and a thousand other sacrificial gifts with love written all over them.

Each of these gifts was a gift of creation, part of the process of helping the child become what we believed God wanted. In a very real sense, Arlie and I teamed up with the Lord to create a baby, then to continue the lifetime of creation.

You who have been involved parents know what I mean when I say that parenting costs—from the time of conception until you die. Parenting costs money, time, personal involvement, giving up things you want to do. There is a sense in which you suffer through all this because you lay down your life to make it happen. Your life is no longer your own. But look what you are helping God create!

Suppose God had established another system. Instead of pregnancy and birth, factories produced babies for parents to buy. Instead of rocking them to sleep, giving 2:00 A.M. feedings, tying shoelaces, and attending soccer games, we delegated all these matters to robots. They did it all for us.

I can't speak for your family, but I can for ours. We are a close-knit family with deep feelings for one another. This delightful friendship was established not by having a robot take care of our children, but by the bonding that took place through the years—brick by brick, day by day, hour by hour. Strong personal relationships were built when we prayed together, laughed together, ate together, sang together, hiked together, and had fun or hurt together. Who wants to have a robot do all these with your children?

God and you teamed up in the creative process. Together you help to make something that will have lasting and lingering benefits for generations to come.

WOUNDEDNESS

Participating in the Cross En Route to the Crown

Almost seven years have passed since Arlie and I shivered in the Adirondack phone booth, listening to unbelievable words that our son had been ripped from the family tapestry in an auto accident. I have heard that time heals wounds, but I do not believe that is true. Time covers wounds, applies a Band-Aid over them, perhaps even a thin scab over them. They become less visible. But the wounds remain. What we have is not a scar, a symbol of healing, but bleeding wounds, if not bleeding externally, bleeding internally.

If you are still grieving for the loss of someone important to you and wonder why, be assured you are a member of the Fellowship of the Wounded. You, like I, will always be wounded. Skin heals but hearts do not. But as we have discussed earlier, while the wound does not heal, we seek new ways to be whole again, a new wholeness that embraces our woundedness, and not only embraces it but uses it to help us become more effective servants of God.

I believe my wife and I will always be wounded because we will always bleed for our son. If we heal completely it suggests we are over it, and I honestly hope that I never reach the point where I am over it, because then I will no longer miss him, no longer grieve for him, no longer pay tribute to him and what he brought into our lives. No, we really do not want to get over it.

But we do want to be changed people, whole people again. Our wholeness does not embrace a living son, as it once did, but memories of a living son. It embraces a desire to make our son's life worthwhile, redemptive.

We do not grieve for what our son is today, or where he is today, for we are assured that he is with God in heavenly places. The promises of the Scriptures present the Way clearly, and Doug had accepted the Way, Jesus. So we do not grieve that he is in heaven. Perhaps we grieve that he is not here on earth with us. That is a bit selfish, I suppose, for the grieving is for us rather than for him. Would we really want to call him from God's kingdom of light, back into this world of darkness? What a devastating blow that would be to someone who has already breathed celestial air, and lived in the presence of the Lord himself.

At times we grieve a bit when we think of what Doug might have done with another sixty years or more. He was a handsome, talented young man. During the last ten years of his life he accomplished exciting things. There were enormous promises. We must guess now what those promises might have produced.

Of course he does not need all that productivity now. No, it won't change his status for eternity one bit. But the world needed it. I think we should grieve for the world because it has missed something very good. We grieve also because we would have enjoyed seeing it happen.

At times I grieve because Doug missed seeing his nieces and nephews. He loved children. I can see him playing on the floor with them. They would have loved him. So I grieve because he missed that, and they missed knowing him.

I grieve at times for all the new adventures our family would have had with Doug. We sense his absence at Christmas, on Turkey Run weekend, on his birthday. For several years our entire family met for dinner on Doug's birthday, to pay tribute to him, to remind ourselves that we have not forgotten. We grieve because he is not there when special days come. He would have added his inimitable sense of humor and robust laughter. He would have made these days more fun.

At times I grieve when I think of the family Doug might have had. I watch my other children and their beautiful mates and wonder who Doug would have chosen. What children would he have today? I grieve because these were children who might have been but never will be. Doug's memory is an image of what was, his wife and children are images of what could have been.

You may perhaps be grieving for these kinds of things too. Sorrow for what could have been, if ... I suppose it is not wrong to grieve for the things we missed, for what could have been, for what we do not have but would like to have, if only ...

But these moments of grief mostly revolve around us. I would like to have seen Doug married to a lovely Christian lady. I would like to have seen his children and played with them. But I would never recall him from his heavenly home, if I could, even for this.

When Joe and Marylou Bayly visited us at the funeral home, Joe said, "Remember, he will always be twenty-six." In my mind, that is true. He remains ageless here in our memory while we grow older. If he were alive, he would be growing older with us, but in our memories, his age is frozen for as long as we live. I can't see him growing older because he doesn't grow older. Age is a product of time and time is a product of living on earth. Beyond twenty-six, Doug did not live on earth. Joe was right, he will always be twenty-six. When Arlie and I are eighty, we will not think of Doug as fifty. We will see him in our minds as twenty-six. But that, too, has a dimension of grief, for we cannot see him maturing through the seasons of life.

Should I grieve that Doug's death cost God something? God places each of us here for a purpose. When we commit ourselves, we minister to him. Doug would have ministered to the Lord for the next fifty years or more. Did his death cost God some important ministry? Perhaps God grieves with me for that missing ministry and the ministries born from his ministry.

These are continuing griefs. I don't dwell on them. They do not consume me. But they will not go away. These, and many others, will reside in my heart throughout my years on earth.

Is it wrong to continue to grieve this way? I think not. Jesus said, "Those who mourn are fortunate! for they shall be comforted" (Matt. 5:4 TLB). Was he talking about this kind of mourning as well as mourning at the graveside? Was he telling me that comfort is the result of mourning for what might have been as well as what was?

For those of you who mourn, do not shrink from true mourning. You may indeed be fortunate, not because you have something to cause you to mourn, but because in your suffering you will encounter comfort. I think what Jesus is telling us is this: When you have suffered loss, mourn! Don't hold back. Someone said that we must bury our dead (or those lost in some other way) or we will carry them like an albatross throughout our lifetimes. In other words, if you refuse to mourn you will always carry the burden that mourning could have removed from you. I think that is what Jesus is saying. Mourning removes the burden that loss placed upon you. Comfort is the relief you enjoy when that burden is lifted. Could we rephrase Matthew 5:4, "Those who mourn are fortunate, for they shall discover the relief of having their burden of loss lifted." The loss is not lifted, but the burden imposed by that loss is.

Each time we mourn, we expose our bleeding wounds again. We take up our personal cross again. But we can learn something about crosses from Jesus. Without the cross, there would be no crown. He did not begin redemption with the crown, he began it with the cross. Jesus came to fulfill a plan of redemption, the crown, but the road to the crown lay through the cross.

I did not seek my suffering, losing my son, but now that it is here, I want to make it redemptive. Like Jesus, I want this cross, this suffering, to be redemptive to others.

TURN YOUR WOUNDS INTO WONDERFUL RENEWAL

Submitting to Life's Surgery to Hasten Healing

When I was a boy I often helped my father on the farm. Those were the days before combines, the modern self-propelled harvesters that farmers now drive through a grain field to harvest a crop in one operation. My father, instead, hitched horses to a binder, a rather innovative machine that cut stalks of grain, gathered them into bundles, tied a string around each bundle, and deposited it on the ground.

Our task as growing children was to gather these bundles and form little stacks that resembled straw igloos. Two or three sheaves of grain laid across the top to help shelter the stack from rain until threshing day. Then on threshing day horses were hitched to a large wagon called a hayrack, open on both sides but enclosed on the ends, and some of us disassembled these little stacks, depositing the sheaves onto the hayrack. The horsedrawn hayrack carried the load of sheaves to the large stationary threshing machine that beat the grain from the stalks.

One hot summer day when we were gathering sheaves in the field, I began to feel wretchedly sick. I had not felt well that morning, but farm people do not stop working merely because they do not feel well. As the morning wore on, I became increasingly nauseated, with pains growing in intensity in my abdomen. At last I could stand it no longer and told my father about my sickness.

When we were able to get to a doctor in the nearby village, he told my father to rush me to the hospital, twenty miles away. My appendix had already ruptured and must be removed immediately.

The surgeon's responsibility was clear. He must cut me open with a knife and cut out the warring member, now exacerbated with gangrene. But wait! I came to the doctor to be healed, not to be wounded. Why was he cutting me open with his knife? Why couldn't he just heal me?

Somewhere I have read of the hypothetical case of a visitor from another planet descending to a modern surgical ward. What would this alien think—white-cloaked people laying a victim on a table, gassing him until he is senseless, then cutting, snipping, and gouging this victim, leaving him not only helpless and senseless, but bloody and wounded. Why cut up a person who has come for help?

Needless to say, I did not ask my surgeon such a foolish question. Nor did my father or mother. We were all happy for the doctor to cut open my abdomen, to wound me with his knife. That was the only way he could help me get well. There was no other option.

The doctor became a wounder. His practice is the art of healing, but healing through wounding. Doctors must do that. They cut us, stick needles in us, hammer on our knees, inflict pain in seeking to alleviate it, and sometimes break bones to reset them so they can heal properly. They are healing wounders.

But there are also wounded healers. You and I may be that kind of person. Because we have been wounded, we carry in us that certain something, a balm of healing possibility, that will help restore other wounded people. Jesus serves in both roles, as a wounding healer and as a wounded healer. As a wounding healer, he sometimes leads us on paths of thorns for our restoration. Sometimes through his Word, he cuts deep into our heart with therapeutic words. Do you remember Jesus' conversation with Peter by the Sea of Galilee? Jesus asked Peter three times if Peter loved him. By the third time, "Peter was grieved" (John 21:17 KJV). Jesus hurt him, but it was for his restoration.

In Isaiah 53 we see Jesus as the wounded healer. There he was, the one willing to be wounded for our redemption, for our wonderful restoration. We will discuss this toward the end of the chapter.

Lifechanger 19
There is healing in our wounds,
for only through our hurts are we able
to help others be healed.

When our friend Ray Christensen died, his wife, Julie, asked me to come to North Carolina to preach the funeral sermon.

After the funeral Arlie and I returned to Julie's home, and as usual, friends and family gathered with food and comfort. As several of us stood in the kitchen with Julie, I mentioned to her, "Julie, because you have been wounded, you will now become a healer."

"That's already happened," Julie responded. Then she told of people in the hospital during Ray's last days gravitating to her for comfort and help, even in the midst of her pain. Jean Bergwall, whose late husband, Evan, had been president of Taylor University, was standing nearby and told of the many people who came to her for comfort since she had lost her husband.

When we're hurt we want to seek the counsel of someone who also has been hurt. We don't want to talk to someone who has merely read about hurt or has heard about it only from others. No, the wounded gravitate to other wounded people for counsel and encouragement. Is it the weak searching for the weak? I think not. I think it is those with recognized weakness seeking those with recognized strength born of weakness. The weakness of woundedness becomes a strength in the eyes of other wounded people.

Could it be that when we are wounded we find personal identity with others in the Fellowship of the Wounded? Do we recognize that only someone who has been hurt will truly empathize with our hurts? Woundedness is not something we can understand merely by reading about it or hearing about it. We must experience it.

Through the years since we lost Doug, I have returned many times to Isaiah 53 to read about the wounded healer so beautifully described there. Isaiah's description of the Man of Sorrows was, of course, a prophecy about Jesus, the wounded Messiah, the Suffering Savior. The image is of someone whose mission is to heal the nations and each of us personally. He would not render his healing through carefully developed prescriptions or sophisticated medicines. Unlike modern surgeons, he would not bring our ultimate healing by further wounding us (although he does this for intermediate healings) but through his own woundedness, his own bleeding. He would become the wounded healer. "By his wounds we are healed" (Isa. 53:5).

I have pondered this matter of wounded healing and in my search have found that I am not alone, for many others have wrestled with this magnificent truth. My struggle, and perhaps yours, focuses on the simple question, "How do wounds heal, especially the wounds of another?" It is related to the question, "How does weakness strengthen?" or "How does death bring life?"

The question of life from death is the easiest of the three for me to visualize because it is exemplified so much in nature. I return to my farm days again and see a grain of wheat die and decay to produce a wheat plant, and later see the wheat plant die and become mutilated to relinquish its grain, which in turn will die and decay to produce another plant. That's easy to see because it's everywhere around us. Trees crash to the forest floor, die and decay, providing fertile ground for another new tree to arise. Parents put life on the line to give birth to children and then invest their lives to raise them so that they will take over the responsibilities of a new generation, which also produces parents who follow the same cycle.

I think all three of these difficult truths are really one, a struggle with identifying what is true power against apparent power, true strength against apparent strength, true life against apparent life. The visible signs of strength are not in reality the essence of true strength. Positions of power, for example, may be personally debilitating, not strengthening.

I know men who were earnest Christians until they gained positions of power and wealth. Then they were corrupted. Outwardly they appeared strong, but inwardly they were rotting. The outward strength they projected was the very thing that corrupted them, made them weak. I'm thinking of one particular man who went through this strength-to-weakness cycle. Ultimately he lost the respect of Christian peers, he lost his wife, he lost the respect of his children, and he lost his desire to please God. Like Samson, this man was outwardly a giant, but inwardly a spiritually degenerating weakling.

What would this man be today if twenty years ago he had lost his job, contracted a debilitating disease, been thrown into prison, or suddenly found himself in the depths of weakness? I don't know, but I know what I would have done. I would have crawled on my hands and knees before God and begged him to restore me to his favor. I rather think that might have happened to this man too. I think if he had been forced into outward weakness, he might today be a giant inside.

Isaiah portrays the coming Messiah, not as a figure of international power, a commanding potentate, but as a Suffering Savior. He painted a picture of a wounded man. But he concludes his portrait of this Man of Sorrows with God's evaluation. "My righteous Servant shall make many to be counted righteous before God, for he shall bear all their sins. Therefore I will give him the honors of one who is mighty and great, because he has poured out his soul unto death" (Isa. 53:11–12 TLB).

Jesus would lay aside divine privilege to identify with human suffering, so that we could ultimately lay aside human suffering to identify with divine privilege. Jesus would give up heaven for a time so that we could enjoy heaven for eternity. Jesus would be wounded so that we could be healed. Jesus would die so that we could live. Jesus would accept our penalties so that we could go free.

To be godly does not mean we are to be otherworldly, angelic, or walk with halos over our heads. It means that in this world we are more Christlike, more willing for our humanness to be wounded so that others might be healed.

Lifechanger 20
Healing comes from the wounds of forgiveness, by forgiving yourself and the person who has wronged you and by "forgiving" God, removing your grudges against him.

"I don't know what I would do if anything ever happened to Mark," Vera McCoy often said concerning her thirty-eight-year-old son. Vera's husband had died of cancer, her younger son died of muscular dystrophy, and her married daughter lived far away in Texas. Mark was the only one at home with her and that was only because he and his wife were separated.

One Wednesday evening in 1985 when Vera left for midweek prayer meeting at her church, she glanced back at Mark, involved in a phone conversation. It was the last time she saw him alive. That evening she was interrupted twice at the prayer meeting, once to say that Mark had gone with a neighbor friend, Frank, to his wife's home to resolve a quarrel between her and her father, Charles. The second time Frank was at the back of the church.

"Let me take you to the hospital," Frank told Vera gently. "Charles shot him." That shot was fatal.

Vera's first instinct was to hate the man who had shot her son. But she made a vow to God that night that she would not sink to hate. "I knew it would destroy me," Vera said later.

One morning, Vera was startled with the thought that she should forgive Charles. Of course she resisted it, and although she began to pray for Charles, she was in a state of limbo between hatred and forgiving. But the day came when she knew she must go to the prison and forgive him.

When Vera saw Charles coming toward her at the prison, she held back the surging thoughts concerning her son, the funeral, and Mark's fatherless boys. Then Vera and Charles stood alone.

Charles hugged Vera and tears came to his eyes. Then Vera took Charles's hand. "I want you to know that I have forgiven you," she said softly, surprised at the peace that engulfed her. "Understand that this does not take away my grief over what has happened, but at the same time, I forgive you."

Vera McCoy continues to be active in the ministry of Prison Fellowship, as she was before her son was killed. Her story is one of remarkable forgiveness, for through her forgiveness of the man who killed her son, she has brought healing to herself and to many whose lives she touches.

An unforgiving spirit is an enormous millstone that we carry around the neck of our souls. Call it what you want—a grudge, spite, revenge, animosity, hostility, malice, resentment, a desire to get even—it all amounts to a burden that prevents us from unencumbered living. It is a weight that drags us down and robs us of the freedom of joyful living.

The Man of Sorrows described in Isaiah 53 was not only a Suffering Savior, but also a Forgiving Savior. On the cross, Jesus said concerning his tormentors, "Father, forgive them; for they know not what they do" (Luke 23:24 KJV).

Being wounded for sinners was not enough. This Suffering Savior must forgive those who were wounding him. Without forgiveness, his woundedness would not have been *for* them, (or us, since vicariously we were one of them). It would merely be woundedness. Nothing more.

Jesus' woundedness paid the price for our restoration. His forgiveness stamped the debt incurred by sin "clear and paid." His woundedness spoke of the descent of God into human suffering, but his forgiveness spoke of the ascent of restored man into divine acceptance.

The incarnation identified Jesus as God *with us.* The crucifixion identified Jesus as God *for us.* The resurrection identified Jesus as God *restoring us* to life as he intended it to be in Eden. The ascension identified Jesus as God *preceding us* to the home he planned for us before the foundation of the world. Without the incarnation Jesus could not have been wounded. Without the crucifixion Jesus would not have been wounded. Without the resurrection Jesus' woundedness would not have been for our restoration. Without the ascension Jesus' woundedness would not have bridged earth and heaven.

Jesus' forgiveness and our forgiveness are in one sense cut from the same piece of cloth but viewed from opposite sides. Jesus' forgiveness removes our sin. Our forgiveness cannot do that. Jesus' forgiveness cancels our debt against him. Our forgiveness cannot do that either.

When we forgive another person, as Vera McCoy did, we remove the burden of revenge, punishment, or retaliation we hold against that person. What we remove is not the other person's sin but our own burden, our anxious desire to see that person get what is coming to him. We do not erase the sin against us, but we erase the cry for justice. Mercy transcends justice, and in that moment we transcend the human demand for justice and accept the divine plan for mercy. In that we become godly, Christlike.

When we forgive ourselves, we cannot erase our own sin either. But we erase the demand for punishment that we have inflicted upon ourselves, we substitute mercy for justice even for ourselves, and thus we erase the guilt feelings that have plagued us for so long, the old feelings that have kept us at war with ourselves and caused self to depreciate self.

When we "forgive God" we obviously do not tell God that his sins are forgiven. How ludicrous! Nor do we show mercy to God. But the grudge we have carried is a grudge we have held against God. Perhaps we think that God killed our loved one, or that he engineered our bankruptcy, or that it was his doing that flooded our home or sent a raging windstorm to destroy us.

God cannot sin, so there is no sin to forgive. The sin is in our grudge against God. It is a grudge that is keeping us from a fully happy life. We sin against ourselves and against God with that grudge. "Forgiving God" is nothing more than erasing the stupid grudge we hold against him. We no longer hold him accountable for what happened. We no longer blame him for our downfall, our agony, our wounds. We erase the unwarranted charge we made against him, and in doing that we remove the burden and we are healed.

In one sense to forgive is to be wounded. It hurts us to remove the penalty from the other person, to cancel the debt we established in our mind against him. But that woundedness is for *our* healing as well as for the other person's healing. We are not truly healed until we forgive. Our forgiveness heals a wounded relationship, a wounded spirit in us, and exhibits a Christlike spirit to those who observe us. And it is that Christlike spirit in us that attracts those who hunger and thirst for righteousness to Christ himself.

Lifechanger 21
*We are restored by identifying our wounds
with the wounds of the Suffering Savior.*

About a year before he died, Doug bought an old pump organ and told us that he would restore it as a gift to us. It was a loving act, and one that cost him dearly. I don't know how many hours he invested in that organ, or should I say how many hours he invested in us. He gave up time that he could have used for his own pleasure, or to earn money, but he knew that we wanted an antique pump organ for our home and those fully restored were prohibitively expensive.

I watched Doug take the organ apart. He took the marred walnut wood to be stripped, then applied seven layers of finish, carefully sanding and rubbing each one. He removed the pedals and had them plated with brass. He ordered magazines and catalogs so he could understand what parts to buy and where to buy them. Then he carefully restored each broken part, even remaking the entire bellows system. It was a painful process, but I think he enjoyed it, not because he wanted the organ, but because he wanted us to have it. It was a gift of love.

I often look at the beautiful restored organ now and think of his gift of time and talent and love. In a very real sense Doug suffered for us, was wounded for us, so that we might have this beautiful instrument.

But I often feel wounded when I see the organ, not that I regret what he did, but that I somehow participated in all his suffering, his wounding, to give us that gift. I believe I understand better now our participating in the wounds of Jesus, and his participation in our wounds. I learn to hurt with Jesus, to feel the pain needed to be his disciple, just as he hurt with me because of my sin.

Jesus came to participate in human suffering, to hurt with us. But to become a Christian is to participate in Jesus' suffering, to hurt with him. His suffering on the cross was a participation in our sinful condition, descending into it that he might take us out of it. But our commitment to be his disciple is a commitment to follow in his steps, even when they lead to the cross. As Christians we do not merely stroll along with him in the pleasant paths of Galilee (or your hometown) but ascend with him on a path of thorns to Calvary.

Isn't that what Paul was saying, "That I may know him, and the power of his resurrection, and the fellowship of his sufferings" (Phil. 3:10 KJV). We know Christ intimately as we participate, or fellowship, with him in his sufferings, just as he participated in our sufferings.

The psalmist said concerning the Shepherd Lord, "He restoreth my soul" (Ps. 23:3 KJV). Restoration is renewal, setting things in order again. The old organ was restored when Doug completed his work, it was in order again as the manufacturer had planned. It functions as the manufacturer specified, looks like it did under the manufacturer's care, and brings forth the beauty of music that was in the mind of the maker.

I believe our restoration from our woundedness comes as we participate in our Lord's woundedness. He alone can "restore our soul." I am whole again not because I have found a better self-improvement program, but because I have found a Suffering Savior who was wounded for me. As I participate in his woundedness for me, so then I shall participate in his resurrection glory, where life is fully restored, in order with the Creator's specifications, in line with the Creator's purposes, fit at last for his eternal home.

I will not go out looking for hurts, but when they come, I will seek to identify with the hurting Jesus. Then I will ask him to "restore my soul."

Lifechanger 22
We prepare for hurts best by preparing our minds and hearts before they come and not by waiting until they come.

One moment I stood in an Adirondack phone booth, inserting coins, expecting a happy conversation with our family at home. The next moment I was a broken man, with news of the death of my son. Only a few seconds separated my two vastly different situations.

Years ago some neighbors left on a family outing. These were fun-filled adventures, usually. But while they were driving along, a truck jumped into their lane and the entire family was wiped out in a moment.

Planes go down with only seconds, if anything, for people inside to prepare for death. Auto accidents usually don't give timely warnings. They happen instantly. For that matter almost anything that can be called an accident is instantaneous.

I found it immensely helpful to have settled certain things in my own mind before Doug's accident. I can't imagine the turmoil of mind if I had to sort out all of these things in the moments after the news came to me. I believe if you settle the following matters that I had settled, and perhaps more, in your more tranquil moments, instant tragedy will be much less difficult to accept:

1. God is in control of his universe. Nothing happens without his knowledge and permission. God knew all of the circumstances and events and thoughts and intents surrounding Doug's accident.

2. God does not direct every tragedy or accident. He permits certain things to happen, but he doesn't necessarily make it happen. God establishes certain laws which guide our universe. Sometimes these get out of hand such as a hurricane that demolishes your home or a tornado or a flood. His laws short-circuit at times, just as his people do.

3. At times, God intervenes with a miracle. Biblical and Christian history is filled with them. But miracles are exceptions to the rules God established. Before I ask for a major miracle, I should recognize that there are good reasons why God may not want to grant my request. For example, I may pray for dry weather so I can go to a ball game, but it may deprive farmers of needed rain. My "miracle" would be selfish, and God is not in the business of sending miracles for selfish purposes.

4. There may be reasons for some hurts that I will not understand because the explanation wouldn't make sense this side of heaven. I must trust God with things that are beyond human understanding. He sees infinitely more than I do.

5. God is good (see Nahum 1:7). Evil never comes from God. If something is truly evil, it did not come from God. It could not come from God. We can never blame God for anything that is truly evil. Some things that we may think are evil are not. God may indeed send short-term hurt to give us long-term help, and we may mistakenly think the hurt is evil because it hurts. But it is actually good because it is for our benefit. Pain or suffering of itself is not evil. Before I label something evil, I must first ask what good could come from it.

6. I will trust God no matter what happens to me or my loved ones. That is because God is trustworthy. He really does know what he is doing. God's greatest desire is to lovingly help us, not hurt us, even though he must hurt us momentarily in order to help us ultimately.

7. *God is my ultimate help in time of trouble.* I would be most foolish to turn my back on God or blame him for my trouble. He is the one I need most to guide me through my hurts.

8. *Love is sacrificial.* God's Son was willing to die for me, not because he had to, but because he loved me. I have decided that I am willing to die for my wife, my children, my grandchildren, if ever I must. The decision at that moment would not be an agonizing one because I have already made it. If I am not willing to die for them, I may not love them enough.

9. *I do not know at what moment I may be taken from this world without warning, without a second to change.* I have confronted my own sin and my need for a Savior and have accepted Jesus as my Savior. I have asked him to forgive my sins. I feel secure that I am ready to go if I should die instantly.

10. *After God, the most important people in the world to me are my family members.* They deserve my highest priority and will receive it. When Doug died, I felt consoled that there were not many things I wished that I had done for him, with him, but hadn't. There are always a few, of course. I always wanted to set up a workshop and build something like a canoe with my sons. We didn't do that. But there were many other things that we did together that were not on my priority list, so I suppose it balances out.

11. *When I get hurt, I am not an exception to the human race.* Others get hurt too. When I am tempted to ask, "Why me?" I may as easily ask, "Why not me?" God is not picking on me, although when hurts bunch up it may seem like it.

12. Every hurt has redemption written on the other side. It is my choice to sit in the corner and cry my life away, curse God, and eat bitter herbs, or to step forth with my pain visible and seek healing for myself and for those about me.

These have been helpful guidelines for me. There may be others. I trust they may be helpful for you. Of course you will have your own unique guidelines also.

If you have not settled matters such as these, I would urge you to form settled convictions concerning them soon. Please do not wait until tragedy strikes and then try to sort out matters of such consequence while you are also sorting out grief. It's too much to handle at the time of crisis. That's why many people cave in when tragedy strikes. They have left too much unresolved for the crisis moment.

Lifechanger 23
The wounded in church or society are our national treasure. They have "healing in their wings," and we must encourage them to apply it to other hurting people.

There is an upside down idea running loose—make yourself look strong by making others look weak, make yourself look big by making others look small. Unfortunately many of us are anxious to look as strong or as big as we can. So we succumb to the temptation to downgrade others, thinking that will upgrade us. Sometimes husbands and wives, or parents and children, sink into this trap. We wound people who love us most in a most unloving way because we selfishly love ourselves more than them.

I have seen this way of thinking in places where I have worked, haven't you? Drop a little hint that depreciates a fellow worker. Make the other fellow look bad whenever you can. If this is true in the workplace, politics is wretchedly filled with it. I'm writing this as a national campaign progresses and am filled with disgust at the candidates as they throw mud at each other. It has become a national sport to ridicule our national leaders for political purposes. This is the kiss of death for any nation. We can't afford it.

It's possible that you may be a victim of some of these tactics. You know how demeaning it is to your personhood. It's especially demeaning when you develop a trust for people only to have them betray your trust. I've had that happen to me, and I'm sure you have too. We need to guard against doing it to others. I only hope that I haven't.

Our society tends to reject the "weak": widows, elderly, handicapped, disadvantaged, minority races. Society sets forth the myth that value depends upon economic productivity. The less a person contributes to the economy, the less his value and more disposable that person is. Productivity is perceived strength and thus woundedness is perceived weakness.

Perhaps that is why these "weak" people often hide. They do not feel needed or wanted. They feel they have less value than before they were wounded. Help them come out of hiding to become healers of other "weak" and broken people. They have something that "strong" people, those who don't see themselves as wounded, do not have.

Lifechanger 24
*Team up with God to become a co-creator
with him.*

We writers are often called creative people, that is, we put words together in ways that we hope have not been done before. We rephrase ideas in unique ways. Occasionally we come up with an idea that we think is new, that no one ever thought of before. Actually, I suspect that there are not that many brand-new ideas around. Our creativity is exhibited in taking the same old words and ideas and giving them fresh garments. Many of the ideas in this book have been around since Bible times. I hope that I am able to restate them and put them into new light so that they have new meaning for you.

I'm always somewhat embarrassed when someone says, "He's the creator of this product." I feel like I must say, "Small *c*, not capital *C*, please."

And yet there is an important dimension of life known as the creativity of personhood. God creates from nothing. We merely establish new form, new meaning, new application, new value to something already there. When we deal with the creativity of personhood, it is necessary for us to team up with God so that he does his work and we do ours. God created people. But he allows us to team up with him in reshaping our wholeness of personhood when we have been broken.

It was God's creative genius that designed personhood. He enlarged the boundaries of my personhood, and yours, to include himself and significant others. When one of those significant others is removed, God gives us the grace and strength to team up with him in re-creating our personhood so that it will be whole again with that significant other removed. It is not easy because it requires a co-creation task. But God and we become co-creators to assure the wholeness of personhood again.

Several years ago Arlie and I sat in Edman Chapel at Wheaton College, listening to the majestic strains of Handel's *Messiah*. It was an occasion to dress up, and we were enjoying every minute of it, not merely because of this wonderful music, but because our daughter Kathy was a cellist in the orchestra.

As we listened to the words, we recognized them as the majestic words from the Book of Isaiah. They were not new, but their musical context was. Of course Handel did not come up with new musical notes, or even new musical technique. Every note was already established as a note. But when Handel put them all together something wonderful happened. He was truly a creator (small *c*). His package of words and notes stirred new meaning in me, evoked new responses in me. In a certain sense, I have often thought of Handel teaming up with God to produce *Messiah*. How could such majesty come from the mind of man?

If Handel were here today, he would probably not try to write some of the books I write. Nor would he likely attempt to overhaul my car engine (neither would I!). Neither he nor I would attempt to build a house. I have some friends who are carpenters and craftsmen, and I admire their creative abilities.

I think each of us has certain creative abilities within us. Arlie dazzles us all with her homemaking abilities. The family owes her an enormous debt for her ability to make home a haven with wonderful sights and sounds and smells that pull us together as a family. It is a creative gift. If you are a full-time homemaker, thank God for your creative talents. Use your creativity as Handel or Mozart used theirs. Theirs are no more important than yours, merely different, more visible to a wider audience, but not more important.

During the last two years, I have served on two time-intensive committees in our church. We formed a future directions committee and met one night each week for almost four months to determine the character of our church, its mission, and its resources. Following that, our church set forth to search for a replacement for our youth pastor, who left to go to seminary, and a new third pastor. I became part of the search committee, which met each Monday night for almost two years. We found the pastors, and now we know that the work was worth it all.

During these two years our committees reaffirmed our church as a "gift-oriented" church, that is, all pastors and lay people in leadership should be in positions that maximize their gifts, and these should be people whose gifts maximize the positions they hold. We think this is the best way to bring creativity, a wide range of creativity, into the best use. In a very real sense this helps team all this creative talent with God's creative genius. God and his people are co-creators in his work.

One of the gifts that is important in a church, or community, is the gift of woundedness. Wounded people have been given a particular gift. For some, it is an added measure of compassion, for others, insight into loss. For still others, there is a special understanding in the whole matter of woundedness. Urge your hurting people to come out of the corner, come out of hiding, and exercise the gifts of healing that they have. Urge them to become co-creators with God in restoring broken people. Wounded people have the greater gifts of healing and restoration of brokenness because they have been through it.

It is not enough that we seek to put bandages on broken people. Nor should we merely repair them. The answer to brokenness is the restoration of wholeness, and this means re-creation, remaking, restoring, reviving. We are trying to help broken, hurting people become new people. After all, this is the genius of the gospel, isn't it? "Therefore, if anyone is in Christ, he is a new creation; the old has gone, and the new has come!" (2 Cor. 5:17).

Lifechanger 25
Team up with God in making your hurts for something, and thus participate in his great plan of redemption.

Each Christmas our family engages in a quaint custom. We wrap gifts in bright paper, grace these colorful packages with ribbons and bows and put them under a tree in our family room. On Christmas morning we present these gifts to each other. It doesn't sound like much, but you have probably discovered in this simple custom the remarkable little word I have discovered—*for*.

"This gift is *for* you," we say. "I am doing this special work *for* you." When Doug restored the old pump organ he did it *for* us. When Arlie prepares breakfast or lunch or dinner, she does it *for* the family. When you do the laundry or ironing, you do it *for* others. The entire system of gift giving, and serving others, is *for* something, *for* someone. Grudgingly giving is not *for* anyone or anything. That's why God loves a cheerful giver (2 Cor. 9:7).

I have found new meaning in Isaiah 53 as I have thought of our serving and giving *for* those we love. I have discovered that *for* and *love* are companions on the road of loving service. We give ourselves and our gifts for someone because we love them. There is no other valid reason to do it. If we give to get, it is not for that person, it is for us. It is not a gift of love but a bait to catch a bigger gift for ourselves. Isaiah said of the coming Suffering Savior, "He was wounded *for* our transgressions, he was bruised *for* our iniquities" (Isa. 53:5 KJV, italics mine). Therein Jesus is distinguished from all other professed gods—his gift was the gift of woundedness, and it was *for* us, for our healing. "With his stripes we are healed" (Isa. 53:5 KJV).

If you have been hurt, you of course feel pain. Pain is the thorn of woundedness. It is the sharp point, the raw edge of being hurt. You may wonder why someone you loved has left you, or why you have lost a job, a home, or something else valuable to you, why death claimed a loved one.

In your pain you may feel the animal instinct to crawl into a dark corner and lick your wounds. There is a time for that. But there is a time to emerge from that dark corner, and with your wounds become redemptive, to make your hurting *for* something, *for* someone.

The genius of the gospel is our model, our path from the ugly cross of suffering that we carry to the resurrection crown of victory. There is no way to a crown, a valid crown, that does not lead through a cross. No athlete ever excelled and wore the crown of accomplishment without going through the cross of practice. No great musician, or artist, or writer, or poet, or statesman, or any other person of accomplishment has ever arrived at the crown of distinction without going through the cross of hard work and deprivation.

If you or I expect to be healed easily, or be a healing, redemptive force in the lives of others, it will not be by sitting in a rocking chair and crying our lives away. It will be by serving, by letting our hurts, our woundedness, be *for* something, *for* someone. The ultimate purpose of our serving is not to be healed, but to heal others. But in healing others, we are healed as well.

QUESTIONS HURTING PEOPLE ASK

A time of hurting is also a time of asking. Perhaps you have asked some of the following questions when you have faced your own unique type of hurts. These questions are typical of those asked at times of hurting. They may be used to stimulate discussion in a small group or to stir your own thoughts. In each chapter I have given a very brief response to each question that has helped me, but it is not intended to be the full answer, only a start. It is hoped that these questions will help you and your friends wrestle with your own answers.

Chapter 1

1. If tragedy should strike today, how would I respond to it? Would I have the strength to see my way through it?
2. How could I prepare myself now in case tragedy should come unexpectedly? What issues should I settle concerning my own ability to handle suffering?
3. How are my relationships with my family and friends, and how might I wish those relationships to be different if tragedy should come unexpectedly? If any of my family members should be taken from me unexpectedly, are there things I wish I could have done with them? Are there things I wish I could have changed in my relationship with them? Are there things I have said that I wish I could withdraw or correct? Is there something I should ask one of my loved ones to forgive?
4. Who would you turn to in a moment of tragedy? Would it be those friends closest to you or your own family?
5. What part would prayer play in your life at the time of unexpected tragedy? What would you say to God in your first prayer?

Chapter 2

1. Have you ever experienced "life on a roll," either upward or downward? How did your feelings change as you rolled in one direction or the other?

2. What specific hurts have you experienced this past year? Which were most painful and which were least painful?
3. Were your most painful hurts related to people or things? Why do you think this is so?
4. Do you enjoy the adventure of living? Would you want to reduce the adventure of living that you enjoy to reduce the risk of getting hurt? Why or why not?
5. Did your most aggravating suffering this last year come upon you suddenly or over a longer period of time? How would you have responded if it had come the other way?
6. What would you say to a hurting friend who says, "I'm just too weak to cope with this. I can't do it"?
7. What would you say to a hurting person who says he or she suffers more because of money, poverty, background, or any other circumstance?
8. What would you say to a person who is angry at God because "he created the world with pain and suffering in it"? Suppose this person says that God could have made the world without pain and suffering and this shows that he really doesn't care about us?
9. When tragedy strikes, what is the best answer to "Why did God do it?"
10. Which should we trust more, God, or what people say about God? Why?
11. Is all emptiness in our lives bad? Is all fullness in our lives good? Why not?
12. What do you think Paul meant when he said, "My strength is made perfect in weakness" (2 Cor. 12:9 KJV)? Has this ever happened to you? How?

Chapter 3

1. Are there times when you have felt broken, like a vase shattered on the floor? What brought this brokenness to you and what did you do about it?
2. Who did you reach out to first in your time of brokenness? How did they help you? How did they not help you?
3. Have you made a foolish decision this last year? Is there anything you can do now to alter the effects of this decision? Have you accepted the fact that you can never change the decision itself, only present circumstances relating to it?
4. Have you ever experienced the feeling of a comma at the end of some major event in your life, unfinished business, unanswered questions, an incomplete relationship? Is there anything you can do to change this in your own situation?
5. If you had been in our circumstances, would you have tried to see your son's mutilated body or remember him as he was?
6. Can you think of anything other than forgiveness that can change the consequences of our past? How can forgiveness do that? Can forgiveness actually change the past, or merely deal with the consequences of it?
7. Certain things we do at a time of tragedy, a funeral for example, are for the people left behind, not for the person we lost. Is this true in any way

for persons who are the victims of divorce or other separation? Can you think of some specifics in your own life?

Chapter 4

1. What are some examples of the need for brokenness to precede wholeness?
2. Have you met broken people who released the Lord's fragrance, or the fragrance of their own personhood, because they were broken? What did they do that showed this fragrance or beauty to those about them?
3. How was God a participant rather that a spectator in our suffering? What does this tell you about God and our relationship to him?
4. How does Jesus make the difference when we must cope with our hurts? What can he offer that no one else can offer at a time like that?

Chapter 5

1. How does the music we choose for weddings or funerals have a lasting impact on our lives? Do you know of people whose broken marriages have been reunited by memories of their special music associated with their courtship?
2. How might the loss of a child affect a mother and father in different ways? How might a mother and father help each other when they understand the difference?
3. In what ways does a graveside service emphasize the finality of death? Why is it important for those of us who have lost loved ones to recognize this finality?
4. How are separation and loss related, or do you think they are the same? Are there differences?

Chapter 6

1. The early church was comfortable in Jerusalem until persecution came. But that persecution sent the Christians out to other parts of the nation and the world, and the gospel with them. What do you think they might have said to one another about this persecution? Do you think they saw it as necessary for the spreading of the gospel at first? What does this say to us about the way we handle difficult times?
2. How does losing a person important to you cause you to evaluate who you are and what you can do?
3. Who are some "significant others" in your life? In what way are they actually part of you rather than being totally removed from your own personhood?
4. When you lose a significant other, how does this actually cause you to lose part of yourself?

5. How do we isolate ourselves, knowingly or unknowingly, from people who might enrich our lives? Can you think of some specific examples?

6. What is the difference between wholeness and completeness? Which should you strive for and why?

7. Can you hope to avoid all loss? Can you choose to avoid it? What can you choose to do when it comes?

8. If you had a difficult childhood, or marriage, or other relationship, can you go back and erase what happened? Can you do something now about the way you will respond to that difficult relationship? What?

9. What is the danger of self-pity? Why will it never give you true healing?

10. What is the most serious damage that comes from self-depreciation? What is the difference between humility and self-depreciation? What is the difference between a recognition of self-worth and pride?

11. Why can't you ever get even with someone? Who does revenge hurt the most? Why?

12. What does atonement (at-one-ment) mean? How could atonement or forgiveness help you deal with the hurts you now face?

Chapter 7

1. In what way is absence a presence? How is absence something that is with you rather than something that is not with you?

2. How then can you best cope with absence? Try to fill up the hole it leaves, or some other way?

3. How do our emotions and our reason wrestle with one another as we deal with loss? In what ways have you let emotions win lately? In what ways have you let reason win lately?

4. Is our loneliness more than just missing a person we have lost? What else is it?

5. What is the difference between loneliness and aloneness? How can aloneness be good for us?

Chapter 8

1. Why can't we deal with loneliness by trying to find a substitute for the person we lost? Why can't we fill up a hole that has been made in our lives?

2. How does the loss of a significant other person affect the "undivided wholeness" of ourselves rather than a divided part of ourselves? What do we mean by "undivided wholeness"?

3. Instead of dwelling in the past, on our loss, what should we do? How might this be a therapy for our hurts?

4. What is the difference between losing someone and being abandoned or forsaken by someone? What difference would you feel? How is being abandoned a double loss?

5. Why would you feel more lonely if you had been abandoned than you would if you had lost a loved one?

6. How is the Lord's "withness" the opposite of being abandoned? What does it do for us when we hurt?

Chapter 9

1. If something tragic happened to you, how would you want your loved ones to grieve for you? What would you want them to do about their responsibilities or opportunities for Christian service soon after their loss?

2. Why do you think some young people die when older people who want to die can't? What would you say to an older person who asks that? What would you say to the parents of a child who has died?

3. Should we expect life to be completely fair? What would it have to be to be fair? How might there be something more important in God's eyes than what we think is fair?

4. When you mourn for someone or something you have lost, what do you do? What is mourning? Are you mourning for the loss or for you?

5. Have you ever experienced "layers of pain," increasing pain associated with a loss? Was one layer more painful than the others? How did you deal with these layers of pain? Which did you cope with first?

6. We experienced the postponement of grief in order to deal with a more immediate layer of pain. Have you ever had to postpone grief, or anger, or coping with a hurt in order to deal with another layer of hurt that was more immediate? How did you handle this?

Chapter 10

1. Have you ever wanted to change the way God has established order in creation? How? What would you have changed? What ultimate effect do you think this would have on the world? On your own life?

2. In what ways are we free to choose our own future? In what ways are we not free to choose our own future? How should we commit those things we can't change to God?

3. How are love and suffering related to each other? Is it possible to love without suffering? Why not?

4. How has loving someone brought suffering to you? How has loving someone brought joy?

5. When you suffer because you loved someone, would it have been better never to have loved at all? Why not?

6. How can suffering relate to majesty? Suffering can bring bitterness and defeat, so how can we turn it instead to something majestic?

7. How are love and sacrifice related? Would God truly love you if he never sacrificed anything for you? Can you truly love another person if you never make a personal sacrifice for that person? Why not?

8. How are suffering and creation interwoven? Would you want a world without any pain or suffering or restraint? Why not?

Chapter 11

1. When we have lost someone important to us, how can we become whole persons again, even though the wounds of loss remain with us?
2. When you say that you grieve for someone, or mourn for that person, what do you mean?
3. Should we shrink from valid mourning? Why not? What did Jesus promise to those who mourn?
4. Can you ever reach the crown without going through the cross? Why not?

Chapter 12

1. In what way was Jesus a wounded healer? How does he also wound us so that he can heal us?
2. What are some everyday examples of our need to be wounded before we can be healed? Have you ever experienced any of these? How were you healed through this wounding?
3. Does God ever deliberately hurt us for the sake of making us hurt? Why not? When he does send hurts, what are they for?
4. Should we ever deliberately hurt anyone for the sake of making that person hurt? Why not? Are there times when we can help someone by hurting that person? Do you know of a specific example?
5. Why is there healing for other wounded people in our own wounds? Why do hurting people gravitate to other hurting people? When you hurt, what kind of person do you want to talk with?
6. Is there ever a time to rejoice in another person's suffering? When?
7. What does it mean to be godly? Is there a difference between appearing to be pious and being truly godly?
8. What happens to us when we forgive another person?
9. How can we "forgive" God? What happens?
10. How did Jesus identify with our suffering? How can we identify with his suffering? How does this identification provide a "fellowship" in suffering with him?
11. When is the best time to prepare for a tragedy, or for hurts that will come into our lives? How can you prepare for such a time?
12. Why are hurting people of so much value to our church, community, and nation? What should we do to maximize that value?
13. How can you join with God in a continuing act of creation? What does this creation do for you?
14. How can you make your suffering redemptive? How can you make it *for* someone or something?
15. As you think of a serious hurt that has been bothering you, how can you turn it into healing, or make it redemptive rather than debilitating for you?